Captain Money *and the* *Golden Girl*

Captain Money
*and the **Golden Girl***

The J. David Affair

Donald C. Bauder

Harcourt Brace Jovanovich, Publishers
San Diego   New York   London

Library of Congress Cataloging in Publication Data
Bauder, Donald C.
    Captain Money and the golden girl.
    Includes index.
    1. Securities fraud—California, Southern.
2. Swindlers and swindling—California, Southern.
3. Dominelli, J. David.   4. Hoover, Nancy.
I. Title.
HV6770.A2C24   1985   364.1′63   85-5512

ISBN 0-15-115501-1

Designed by Francesca M. Smith
Printed in the United States of America

    B C D E

When a man's fancy gets astride on his reason; when imagination is at cuffs with the senses; and common understanding, as well as common sense, is kicked out of doors; the first proselyte he makes is himself.

—Jonathan Swift, "A Tale of a Tub"

Contents

Eight pages of photographs follow page 116.

Acknowledgments

In the course of researching and writing this book I interviewed hundreds of people, most of whom prefer anonymity. Eleven people who played key roles in the J. David adventure went over my entire manuscript for accuracy, and they, too, would rather not be identified. My heartfelt thanks go out to all.

John Radziewicz was an absolutely superb editor, and Kathleen Bursley gave valuable advice.

I received moral and emotional support from the people who are most important to me—my wife, Ellen; my mother, Eleanor; and my two sons, Clinton and Russell. To them I dedicate this book.

Author's Note

J. David & Company is no more, but the "J. David affair" continues to unfold. As this book goes to press, many issues and accusations must still be resolved in court.

On March 21, 1985, as part of a plea-bargaining arrangement, J. David "Jerry" Dominelli confessed to fraud; he faces sentencing and up to 20 years' imprisonment. Nancy Hoover remains under investigation for her role in the company. Mayor Roger Hedgecock's trial on conspiracy and perjury charges resulted in a hung jury on February 13, 1985; Hedgecock will stand trial again. Hoover and Dominelli await trial on charges of illegal financing of Hedgecock's 1983 campaign. Numerous civil suits against principals, lawyers, accountants, and others involved in the J. David affair are still being vigorously contested.

Captain Money and the Golden Girl

1

The Establishment-in-Waiting That Couldn't Wait

He had a passion to do well.

She had a passion to do good.

Together, they touted his investment scheme, which bilked a thousand investors of $80 million. He has confessed to planning and running the swindle; her involvement is under investigation. From conception to collapse the scam was pathetically mismanaged—yet it wound up being one of the largest frauds of its kind in U.S. history.

The scheme had high-priced help from respectable, well-connected law, brokerage, accounting, and insurance firms. Without the expertise and the imprimatur of rectitude these institutions provided, it would quickly have come apart.

J. David "Jerry" Dominelli and his lover and business associate, Nancy Hoover, considered themselves in the vanguard of the New Enlightenment—role models for the Yuppies. Heaping contumely on the gluttonous, atavistic establishment they loathed, Hoover and Dominelli created a public profile as rich people who cared, who shared. They fancied themselves as philanthropic. But belying that image, the lovers went on a four-year personal-spending binge that would have embarrassed America's wealthiest families.

The couple had their own Fantasy Island—a tiny isle in the British West Indies. It wasn't a lovers' hideaway. It was a legal and accounting mirage. For tax and regulatory purposes, they told the government that their firm's financial activities were taking place there.

Their investors believed they were making a steady 40 to 50 percent annually on their money. For three years gullible and greedy people from San Diego and Orange counties and from nearby Palm Springs—and in fact throughout the world—were informed that their nest egg had gone up in value every month except one. It was an absurd claim, but there was a platoon of gung ho ex-Marines and assorted other warriors who aggressively peddled this wondrous investment program. Like good warriors, they never challenged the officers giving the orders, and until the scheme collapsed in bankruptcy, few investors challenged the Marines.

Dominelli, the officer-in-charge, even had an officer's title: "Captain Money." Hoover's children named him that because he lavished so much money on them. Fantasizing about spit and polish and brute force, he would frequently chide Hoover, "You'd never make it in the Marines." But actually *he* had been unable to cut it as a Marine.

He was slight of build, pallid, withdrawn, and publicity-shy. His glasses were as thick and foggy as a gin bottle, and they constantly slid down his nose as he spoke. With a weak smile and a limp gesture, he would slip them back in place with his little finger. He also had an acute hearing problem. When someone addressed him, Dominelli would almost invariably respond, "huh?" Until the end few figured out that the hearing problem was very useful—it gave him time to come up with plausible answers. And some questioned that hearing problem. "He had *selective* hearing loss. He didn't hear what he didn't want to hear. But he could hear a pin drop across the room if it served his purposes," says a government prosecutor. Dominelli also suffered from allergies; if he forgot to pop his pills, he was a basket case.

Nancy Hoover would have made a magnificent Marine. She was as tanned and fit as Dominelli was pale and flabby. Almost six feet tall (three inches taller than he was), she had steeled her psyche in her youth by combatting her hard-bitten Navy pilot father. Day after day, she had shot him down with her vivacity—a quick wit, a gift of gab, eternal effervescence, and optimism. She would later use these tools deftly to get her way. "Nancy is a jungle fighter," comments a former employee. "She responds to power."

Hoover had a very short attention span. "Nancy Hoover—it's very difficult to get her to concentrate on anything for any long period of time. She was probably hyperactive as a child, and to some extent continues to be as an adult," says George Mitrovich, a close friend who played a major role in the company. A word with Hoover "would be sliced between two or three telephone calls," continues Mitrovich, claiming that only once, when she was having marital problems, was he able to talk with her at any length.

A Hoover monologue was a stream of non sequiturs. She leapt from topic to topic—and from emotion to emotion—without perceivable bridges. A listener was inevitably bewildered. "One time," recalls a former executive of the company, "I walked into a bar in mid-afternoon and a fellow from the office rushed in. 'Give me a drink. Nancy's driving me crazy,' he said. She'd make people so frustrated they'd have to get away. She was capable of telescoping events. In one hour with her, you would get the full range of human emotions. All your emotions were challenged."

To people on the inside, she was flawed. But to people on the outside, she appeared almost perfect. "Nancy Hoover is outgoing, natural, debonair, as American as apple pie, as genuine as the Stars and Stripes. She is warm, natural, believable, honest, generous to a fault," says Sandra Kritzik, a socialite who knows Hoover well.

"She has a vivacious smile, she's upbeat, generous to everybody . . . to the mailman, to the taxi driver. She used to give one-hundred-dollar bills to her hairdresser and the lift attendant on skiing trips," says a former close personal and business associate. Sometimes her passion to do good deeds would incinerate her good judgment. "When one of her daughter's girlfriends wanted a new car, and her mother wouldn't buy it for her, Nancy gave her one," says the former associate.

Hoover was as aggressively social as Dominelli was antisocial. She would go out jogging, encounter thirty other joggers en route, and invite them all to her house an hour later for a magnificent brunch. She showered gifts on people and not always for a quid pro quo. Often she gave anonymously.

Hoover was uninhibited in many ways, going around her home topless, for example. But Dominelli was painfully reserved about his body. Indeed, he was a bluenose of sorts. One of his commodity trading advisers, Robert Mengar, liked to drop an earthy comment or two in a company newsletter. When IBM brought out its home computer, colloquially called the "Peanut," Mengar wrote that IBM's competitors suffered from "Peanut envy." Dominelli blushed and edited the phrase out.

Politically Hoover was a liberal social reformer in a conservative city. As such, she had been crowned "The Golden Girl" by fellow liberals in the media. If Dominelli had any political philosophy, it was Libertarian. "If they're gonna get me to pay fuckin' taxes, they're gonna have to come get me," he would say in his Chicago street vernacular. His close colleagues—mostly liberal Democrats—considered him a conservative Republican, and he had taken out an ad in *The Chicago Tribune* in 1980 supporting Ronald Reagan. However, Dominelli also poured money into the campaigns of Democrats, no doubt at Hoover's direction. "Maybe you should call him a Libertarian Republican," says a former associate.

Instinctively Dominelli was an anarchist, someone who hated authority. He believed that with a little professional assistance, he could forever keep the despised authorities off his back. Once, a president of one of his subsidiaries promised a regulatory body that Dominelli wouldn't open another office within the next several months. "Fuck 'em. I'll hire a lawyer," Dominelli said. "That was his philosophy of life. He believed that a lawyer or an accountant could get him out of anything, but he often didn't follow their advice," recalls a former financial official of the firm.

Captain Money and the Golden Girl named their company J. David, and for four years it appeared they might convert their fantasies into reality: He would strike a rich vein, and she would strike the vain rich.

Hoover was out to take over and reform the wealthy, tradition-bound ruling class of San Diego, the nation's eighth largest city and easily one of its most conservative. Like many of her fellow liberals and Yuppies, she preached that the San Diego establishment is callous, selfish, and too tolerant of financial scoundrels.

To an extent, she had a point. In San Diego it's sometimes hard to distinguish the landed gentry from the light-fingered gentry. Cozeners—accepted by the ruling establishment—have been preying on San Diego investors for years. They sun themselves on the beaches in the upscale coastal town of La Jolla and ride to hounds in the aristocratic inland community of Rancho Santa Fe. They are indefatigable party-goers, apotheosized almost daily in the society columns of the local newspapers, despite, in some cases, their records of convictions.

And in San Diego, as in many other cities, it's difficult to distinguish the recidivists from the philanthropists. That's because often they are one and the same. The habitual fast-buck operators buy respectability by pouring money into local charities—always with maximum public exposure.

San Diego's financial scoundrels of the recent past have fallen into two categories. There were the acquisitors, the conglomerateurs—those building a massive empire through accounting voodoo and inflated stock. And then there were the fleecers of the innocent—those promising unbelievably high returns to naive investors.

The classic conglomerateur was the revered C. Arnholt Smith, dubbed "Mr. San Diego of the Century" by a local newspaperman. Smith built a conglomerate that operated many of the city's prime businesses—a taxicab firm, a tuna cannery, a luxury hotel, a shipbuilding yard, an airline— and that owned huge tracts of agricultural land. Smith also controlled a bank with $1 billion in assets. The Byzantine paths by which Smith funneled funds from the bank to the conglomerate, and thence to his own pocket, had investigators befuddled for years. In the early 1970s, the U.S. Treasury Department's Comptroller of the Currency described Smith's bank as "self-dealing lending run riot."

Eventually both the bank and conglomerate went under. In 1975 Smith was indicted for manipulating $170 million in bank funds and channeling $27.5 million to himself and his cronies. He only got probation on these federal charges, but in 1979 he was convicted of grand theft and sentenced to prison by the state. Five years later, on November 26, 1984, he began serving a one-year jail sentence. Now in his mid-eighties, he is still adored by many of La Jolla's Beautiful People.

At the time Smith was being tried, another conglomerate, U.S. Financial, was going into bankruptcy and some of its former executives into the slammer. The company, which controlled important San Diego real estate, became a darling of Wall Street. The stock rose from $4.62 a share to $62 as management used every accounting trick in the book—including selling itself its own assets several different times—to overstate its profits. After the crash common shareholders considered themselves lucky to come out with twenty-five cents on the dollar.

During the same period, still another publicly held company, Royal Inns, which owned hotels and restaurants in eighteen states, was bellying up to the bar. This company reported fat profits from building hotels, but lost money *operating* the hotels. The founder, Earl Gagosian, became very rich selling off the artificially inflated stock, often utilizing inside information, charged the bankruptcy trustee. His multimillion-dollar La Jolla mansion overlooking the Pacific became something of a local shrine—celebrated in the press, ogled by the citizenry and tourists.

Richard L. Burns was an acquisitor hailed by the establishment when he brought his R.L. Burns Corporation to San Diego from San Bernardino in 1977. He bought Gagosian's mansion and moved his company into the posh quarters previously occupied by John Alessio—a racetrack entrepreneur, ex–"Mr. San Diego," and C. Arnholt Smith associate who had gone to jail. Like Smith and Alessio, Burns established himself as an eleemosynar, generously donating to local charities. His energy company seemingly prospered, but one day the entrepreneur stunned shareholders by peddling his stock for $14.6 million at a time when it was worth $40 million on the market. Shortly thereafter, as grim news hit, the company and its stock collapsed. Burns used his proceeds to buy another company, Nucorp Energy, and launched an acquisition binge, gobbling up oil-field equipment suppliers with stock that rose 2,100 percent in just two years. But that 2,100 percent gain vanished almost overnight when the company plunged ingloriously into bankruptcy amid a sea of lawsuits.

The Securities and Exchange Commission has charged Burns and a fellow official with inflating revenue by $50 million through the dubious practice of "prebilling": recording a sale on the books at the time of the handshake, rather than after the product is manufactured, sold, and delivered to the customer in return for money. The bankruptcy trustee is suing Burns for $10.4 million, and the company still owes banks $326 million. Not surprisingly, the major bank is Continental Illinois, which has since been, in effect, nationalized because of its bad energy loans. Continental Illinois loaned Nucorp more than $100 million and also loaned large sums to Burns personally.

There were conglomerateurs who kept company with San Diego's rich and chic, but didn't share San Diegans' conservative philosophy. One was Rancho Santa Fe's Walter Wencke, a Harvard-trained labor lawyer who dared to run for Congress as a Democrat. Wencke didn't make it to Congress, but he *is* recognized in government offices throughout the land. His picture, along with those of fellow missing criminals, adorns post-office walls. Wencke, too, built and pillaged a conglomerate, but he had the foresight to keep stashing money in tax-haven banks while his case dragged through the courts.

On October 9, 1979, Wencke was to begin serving a five-year prison sentence for mail fraud and making false statements to the SEC. But he never showed up and has never been found, although every couple of months someone claims to have seen him on some Caribbean isle. The only people to have heard from Wencke have been officials of the Central Intelligence Agency. He wrote them asking for a job not long before he skipped the country, noting, "It would take many individuals with different skills to accomplish what I can do alone."

The conglomerateurs preyed mainly on fellow sophisticates—wealthy and world-wise people who knew what they could be getting into. But San Diego has also had entrepreneurs who specialized in taking advantage of "the little people," particularly the elderly and retired, who make up a significant part of the population. Joseph Anthony Bello promised small investors as much as 120 percent a year in the late 1970s. He eventually went to jail for mail fraud and filing a false income-tax return. Paul J. Boileau sold the elderly high-yielding, speculative housing paper called "second trust deeds" and in 1982 took the Fifth Amendment at his bankruptcy hearing while sitting safely behind a bulletproof shield. Stephen Lochmiller sold high-yielding trust deeds to low- and middle-income retirees and then lent out the money for Palm Springs homes appraised at highly inflated values. More than fifty glowering victims were in the courtroom in 1984 when he was sentenced to four years for selling unregistered securities. Bernard Striar (alias Eldean Erickson) pocketed commodity investors' money instead of investing it—similar to what he had done, it turned out, in several other cities under several other names. Upon leaving town in late 1984, Striar left a plaintive note: "I guess there is no other way to put it, except that I'm a fraud and a crook. . . . The FBI is very familiar with me." He had lasted nine years in San Diego—his longest stretch in any city. He has been arrested and indicted for fraud.

San Diegans not only fall for such rustlers—they fall all over them. Despite the notoriety of past brigands, each new shark to surface is instantly surrounded by investors anxious to get in the swim.

Clearly it was the ideal market for Captain Money and the Golden Girl. They didn't dream small dreams. Dominelli intended to combine the dubious strategy of the little-people fleecer with the dubious strategy of the conglomerate builder. He promised investors returns of up to 50 percent a year, and he also planned to erect a diversified financial giant modeled on Wall Street's Goldman, Sachs.

Some say it could only have been attempted in Southern California. They theorize that the constant sunshine softens San Diegans up for swindlers. The sun, in fact, *is* partially to blame. Because it shines all year, people flock to San Diego. In the last two decades, San Diego has consistently been one of the fastest-growing metropolitan areas in the U.S., and three-fourths of that growth has come from in-migrants. Often there are fifty to one hundred applicants for one job opening, and there are thousands of well-trained, retired military officers on fat pensions who are willing to work for low wages.

Conspicuous consumption is omnipresent. San Diegans buy more Mercedes-Benzes than Plymouths. Housing prices have been pushed sky-high (averaging $133,000), but incomes are only slightly higher than the national urban average. The upwardly mobile must get deeply into debt and then have to come up with big incomes to meet the monthly mortgage.

For many that means taking risks—mortgaging to the eyeballs and rolling the dice. San Diego is full of "high-stakes poker players," notes Howard Matloff, a San Diego lawyer who specializes in white-collar crime. There's no Old Wealth watchdog to keep a lid on the fun. Almost everybody is nouveau riche, and a laissez-faire mentality rules.

Then, there's what Matloff calls "the Disneyland effect." Many people have made a bundle in local real estate. In the late 1970s, average real estate prices in San Diego rose 25 percent a year, and amateurs routinely turned 100 percent profits in real estate deals. Thus, J. David's promise of a 50 percent annual return was not greeted with the skepticism it deserved.

"It all boils down to greed and glitter," says Roger Young, former head of the FBI in San Diego. "All reason goes down the drain. You lose your senses. In the excitement and rush to amass the manna, investors forget to ask, 'What kind of a track record does this promoter have? Where did he come from? Who are his associates? Is the operation audited? Are records available? Will respectable people endorse the promoter? Is the investment registered?' A claim of 40 to 50 percent annual returns is a flag—a tip-off." Other clues, according to Young, include social and financial relationships with prominent politicians and generous, well-publicized gifts to local charitable organizations.

Besides the greed and glitter, there's another factor: San Diego sits on the Mexican border. It's a way station for drugs moving into the U.S. from Central and South America. Drug dealers' money has to be "laundered," that is, transformed into respectable money or credit. Some entrepreneurs with foreign-banking connections will provide this service for a fee of around 10 percent. This means there is always a lot of illicit cash seeking a licit home in San Diego, and that kind of lucre often finds its way into local swindles.

While Jerry Dominelli and Nancy Hoover found the San Diego environment extremely hospitable for their investment scheme, they hadn't gone out of their way to select it as a thieves' haven, as the blue-suede-shoe city-hoppers often do. Hoover had been born in San Diego. Dominelli had discovered it during his military tour.

A document on J. David stationery supposedly spelled out

Dominelli's biography: "Jerry Dominelli was born in Chicago. A graduate of St. Dominic's High School, he served with the United States Marine Corps in Vietnam. Following completion of his military service, he enrolled in the University of San Diego, graduating with a B.S. in economics in 1969."

The biography was largely untrue. Dominelli, born in 1941 and one of six children, had been expelled from St. Dominic's as a sophomore. (In a sworn statement to the SEC early in J. David's existence, Dominelli declared that he was a St. Dominic's graduate, but researchers, checking parish, Marine Corps, and college records, can find no indication of a graduation or equivalency certificate.) His youth had been filled with anxiety. He had been the kid with the thick glasses in an Italian neighborhood teeming with leather-jacketed toughs. He had sometimes walked three blocks out of his way to avoid local bullies, he admitted to friends. It was in this unhappy period that he began fantasizing about getting rich, becoming at least a millionaire by age forty.

After dropping out of high school Dominelli had entered the Marines, but had never been in Vietnam. Nor, as he bragged to his employees and investors, had he been a member of Force Recon, the elite Marine unit that takes to the air (parachuting) and the deep sea (scuba diving) in pursuit of the enemy. It was a dangerous boast in San Diego, aswarm with veterans. After seeing Dominelli just once, a retired Marine general harrumphed, "He has never been in Force Recon." The retired general was correct, of course. (Shrewdly Dominelli never made such boasts to colleagues who had served in Vietnam or been in Force Recon.)

Officially, the Marines say, Dominelli had gone through boot camp at San Diego County's Camp Pendleton and then been sent to Okinawa. For a year he had traveled between Okinawa and Thailand, but not to Vietnam. In fact, he left the Marines in 1963, two years before Marines actually landed in Vietnam. (Up to then there had been only so-called Marine advisers there.) During his service Dominelli had been promoted to lance corporal, but he was discharged, honorably, as a private after unspecified scrapes with authorities.

Despite the lack of a high school diploma, Dominelli had been accepted by the University of San Diego and had graduated with a C-plus average. He had married and become the father of two daughters. He had gotten his first job with Equity Funding, which was later to become immersed in one of the major financial scandals of the 1970s. After a short stay, Dominelli left Equity Funding and bounced from one Southern California brokerage branch to another: H. Hentz; Bateman Eichler, Hill Richards; Shearson Hayden Stone (now Shearson Lehman Brothers); and Bache Halsey Stuart Shields (now Prudential-Bache). Briefly during those years he had studied law at night.

Dominelli's career as a broker had been totally undistinguished. "He was a mediocre broker at best," says John Farrish, his manager at Bache. A former supervisor remembers him as "a disaster as a trader." "He walked around with his head down and seldom spoke to anybody," recalls a colleague of the time. "He was never much of a broker."

Like Dominelli, Hoover was doxologized in J. David's biography: "Nancy Hoover was born in San Diego. A graduate of Pensacola, Florida High School, she took her

Baccalaureate from the University of California–Berkeley, pursuing a career as a foreign service officer, stationed in Brazil and Portugal."

Nancy Hoover did not live up to this biography. She was born in 1938 into a Navy family. She *had* graduated from high school in Pensacola, but she had *not* graduated from Cal-Berkeley—in fact, she had no college degree. The Golden Girl had attended the College of William and Mary and San Diego State, but had left the latter to elope with George Hoover, who went on to become a foreign service officer. She had accompanied him as his wife and the mother of their son and daughter, but she had not been in the foreign service.

Eventually George Hoover had quit to go into the brokerage business, and he, Nancy, and their two children had moved to Del Mar, an affluent coastal community just north of La Jolla. There Nancy Hoover blossomed. She served on the Del Mar City Council for eight years (1974–1982), including one year (1976) as mayor. Championing liberal causes, she incurred the enmity of the powerful construction industry, but won the admiration of the Yuppies by voting for zoning restrictions on valuable property; by supporting environmentalists, feminists, and reformers of all varieties; and by vehemently opposing offshore oil drilling. After brief jobs at the publication *Psychology Today* and at San Diego Securities, she arrived at the La Jolla office of Bache in 1976 as a rookie broker. Her husband was a top producer and administrator there—and J. David "Jerry" Dominelli was a green and not-very-promising broker. Hoover and Dominelli shared a desk in the bull pen, an area reserved for low producers.

For their fellow brokers, the Hoover-Dominelli tandem

provided comic relief. It was Wally Cox teamed with Vanessa Redgrave, J. Walter Mitty arm-in-arm with the Bionic Woman.

To everyone's amazement, Hoover and Dominelli became fast friends—but George Hoover never worried. He considered Dominelli a wimp and a mental lightweight.

One afternoon, Dominelli, Nancy Hoover, and three other Bache brokers (including Robert Kritzik, socialite Sandra Kritzik's husband) held a bitching session over lunch. They talked about forming a boutique brokerage house that would cater to an upscale clientele—serving coffee in fancy china cups instead of cheap Styrofoam containers. Brokers would get higher commissions and be free of the oppressiveness of large New York–based brokerages.

It was 1979 and the middle of a dolorous bear market. Morale was rock-bottom. The idea of breaking away was attractive, but nobody thought the reclusive Dominelli would be the one to do it, even though he suddenly seemed to have money in his pocket. (He said he had been successful in real estate. He didn't mention that his wife, Antje, had received a substantial insurance payment. A woman in an adjoining apartment had committed suicide by turning on the gas, which had leaked next door and killed Mrs. Dominelli's mother and father.)

In mid-1979 George Hoover left Bache to go to the La Jolla office of another Wall Street firm, Drexel Burnham Lambert; a few months later, several Bache brokers joined him. One was Nancy Hoover. But Dominelli quit Bache to go out on his own—to start his own commodities trading advisory. He intended to collect money from customers, put it in a pool or a partnership, and then invest it in commodities like gold, foreign currencies, financial futures, and other instruments.

After only two months at Drexel, Nancy Hoover returned to Bache and told George she was getting a divorce. At Bache she was to become the broker-of-record for Jerry Dominelli's new commodities trading firm. He had opened a tiny office in the basement of a Mexican restaurant in downtown La Jolla. The office was dark and dank, but generally agreeable except when the sewer backed up, as it did on occasion. Bache also gave Dominelli space in its office, even though he was no longer on the payroll. Dominelli called the shots and Hoover placed the orders through Bache. The firm known as J. David was born.

The birth had been preceded by a romance. One Sunday afternoon, two Bache brokers were in the office. Dominelli and Hoover came in barefoot. They had been to the beach and wanted to catch up on work. "I noticed that as they sat at the desk, their toes were touching. I could not believe it. Neither could my buddy," recalls one broker.

By and large it was a discreet affair. In February 1983, the Kritziks, close friends of Hoover and Dominelli, realized for the first time that the two were lovers. Sandra Kritzik went to see an apartment Hoover and Dominelli had purchased and noticed that there was only one bed, and a pink negligee hanging in the bathroom.

From the start Captain Money and the Golden Girl established themselves as workaholics, toiling from early morning to late evening. At the outset J. David collected small amounts—$3,000 or $5,000 or $10,000—from individuals and invested the proceeds. The pools were moderately successful; some made money, some lost money. None did smashingly well or egregiously poorly.

To sell his pools and partnerships, Dominelli distributed throughout San Diego a track record he claimed to have compiled while at Bache. According to the unaudited document, he had started with $5,000 in December 1977 and nimbly put it into gold, Swiss francs, British pounds, and Treasury bonds and bills. By the last day of 1977, the pot had grown to $52,181.50.

The next year, according to the track record, Dominelli had started with $10,000 and adeptly dabbled in foreign currencies, federal paper, copper futures, and the like. By year's end the pot had ballooned to $84,446.85. Through the dog days of 1979, some $15,000 had swelled to $39,592.

By chance a man writing a book on commodities, Mark Robert Yarry, was investing through Bache's La Jolla office at the time. He met Dominelli and studied his track record. So impressed was Yarry that he inserted the record in his book, *The Fastest Game in Town: Commodities,* published in 1981 by Prentice-Hall.

Yarry declared Dominelli—never identified by name as the broker who had compiled the amazing record—a "genius." At J. David, Yarry's book became a sales tool. Soon Dominelli was talked about all over San Diego.

The word most people used was "genius."

"I thought he was an oddball, a kook, an eccentric—but a genius trader," recalls an investor who eventually put more than $1 million with J. David.

"His behavior was bizarre. He was so eccentric. But I thought he was a genius at trading," says another investor, who was paid large commissions to steer his clients to Dominelli.

When the Beautiful People would ask what Nancy Hoover saw in Jerry Dominelli, the reply would almost always be "his brains."

Dominelli's appearance and demeanor helped establish the image. His thick glasses, acute hearing problem, and shyness all somehow smacked of genius. He would abruptly walk out of a tense meeting in mid-sentence, mumbling as he stared into space. "He was the absent-minded professor," says Sandra Kritzik, whose family pumped half a million dollars into Dominelli's operation. "One permits a genius his idiosyncrasies. I really thought Jerry was a financial genius. Had I met him in any other circumstance, I would have thought of him as a nothing."

His language was memorable. "Every other word was 'fuck,'" recalls a former executive. Dominelli would sit at his quote machine watching prices in international currencies change and would sporadically blurt, "Fuckin' franc!"

"He was a street kid with street smarts, but he wasn't articulate," remembers Kritzik. His crudity in public often embarrassed more refined companions, including Hoover.

Almost everyone who knew Dominelli described him as "a nice guy." He appeared to have a frail ego to match his frail stature. He exuded humility. However, as a friend says, "he had a violent temper." Once he was threatening to sue a former employee of the firm. "If this was 1890, I'd shoot him with a fuckin' gun," shouted Dominelli, demanding that one of his vice-presidents get a signed document from the ex-employee. "What do you want me to do? Break his arm?" said the vice-president. "Do anything to get that fuckin' signature," Dominelli told the vice-president and then added, "You're no longer an employee of this company." Later, though, Dominelli relented. "I only said that to you because I was in a room full of lawyers," he explained.

Dominelli was indecisive, but considerate of people who had been hurt by his changes of mind. One Friday a president of a subsidiary finally talked Dominelli into hiring an accountant. By Monday Dominelli had flip-flopped. "We don't need a fuckin' accountant," he said. "Should I tell him to leave? He's right outside the door," replied the executive. "Oh, Christ. Well, OK, get him a desk," shrugged Dominelli.

Dominelli was an enigma to his employees. He overpaid them, lavished them with gifts, and reeked of solicitude; but like Hoover, he had a short attention span and very little time for anybody. As long as people believed that he was an authentic financial genius, however, he had indisputable charisma. "Getting an audience with Jerry was like getting an audience with a king. He captivated people, had a real flair," says a former executive. "Think of Jerry as a chameleon. He can be anything he thinks you want him to be. If he thinks you would like to see him sad, he can come on sad," according to a former officer of J. David.

Dominelli's kindnesses were legendary. When a secretary died, he paid for the funeral. When the daughter of a consultant had a medical emergency and had to be flown out of remote ski country, Dominelli dispatched his personal jet immediately and refused to accept a penny of payment from the grateful father, a man of considerable wealth.

He even took in stray cats. One that occupied his office was named Swissie, after the Swiss franc.

When refurbishing a new J. David office, workmen had set traps for mice. Dominelli couldn't bear to see dead mice in traps; he would spring all the traps, leaving the cheese so that the mice could dine in safety.

One of Dominelli's great weaknesses was that he couldn't refuse requests for money—from local charities, from employees wanting to launch a project, from friends wanting a loan or his participation in an investment. This quality endeared him to Nancy Hoover. And there was nothing in his life more important than pleasing her.

She had divorced her husband because she considered him a pennypincher. "We'd be dining out with people and he would never reach for the tab," she complained bitterly. She dreamed of becoming a great philanthropist, arts patron, and friend of the downtrodden, but could never realize the dream with her husband. "I can't understand people who conserve their money," she told an associate. "What good is it lying in banks?" Money was to be spent and to be given away.

The willingness to part with money quickly—and foolishly—was one of the main things Captain Money and the Golden Girl had in common. "Jerry is the consummate consumer," Hoover would bubble. Their offices were absurdly ornate. They bought $100,000 foreign sports cars by the dozens. Still unsated they bought a limousine company for personal transportation. They had three jets. They owned several elegant homes. They shelled out ridiculously high sums for racehorses. She collected expensive jewelry. He wore only drab but very expensive suits, mostly pinstripe, with vests. At the company's peak, he had fifty such suits, and four dozen pairs of shoes, all Italian wing tips.

To some people, such ostentatious consumption didn't fit with the public image Hoover was trying to cultivate.

"She claims to be a liberal. She's a fourteenth-century French courtesan, for Christ's sake," says a former J. David employee. Many friends believe that Hoover really craved the life of luxury because she was trying to one-up her sister, who had married into a rich establishment family.

But there was the other side of Hoover: She had an uncontrollable obsession to give money away. Before J. David made it big, she had told the local media, "My real dream is that I'd like to help more, if I could get really rich."

According to the J. David biography, Hoover became known as "one of the city's leading arts patrons." *That* wasn't hyperbole. She was. She joined the board of the symphony and the La Jolla Museum of Contemporary Art. She helped the poor and dozens of local causes. Almost no charity was turned down.

Soon, Captain Money and the Golden Girl were celebrated for their lavish parties, attended by local and national politicians, the rich and the chic, and the "new class" of liberals she was grooming for a raid on the establishment. Indeed, the whole J. David clique was thought of in San Diego as "the establishment-in-waiting."

At the parties Jerry Dominelli faded into the background as Hoover luminesced. Sometimes he was introduced as "Mr. Hoover."

Once he was intending to have a private birthday party for himself with one of his daughters at a local inn. Hoover, who was very jealous of Dominelli's wife and children, tried to upstage the get-together by inviting the office for a surprise party at the same inn at the same time. Word of the surprise got to Dominelli just as he was mounting the stairs to the second floor of the inn, where many of his employees, awash in bottled spirits, were waiting to belt out "Happy Birthday." "Goddamned Hoover!" he exclaimed, racing back downstairs. He ducked into a washroom and hid there for some time, leaving his daughter to fend for herself. Later he emerged and reluctantly joined the party.

Generally, he was a willing if timid participant in these parties, as long as he could spend part of his time with Hoover. "Jerry couldn't stand to be separated from her. He was like a teddy bear or a cocker spaniel. He would wander into an area where she was. There was no hugging or physical contact—he just wanted to bask in her aura," recalls Sandra Kritzik. At one skiing party, she injured her hand, so he cut her food for her and fed her with his fork.

At social gatherings Dominelli would soon tire of the glad-handing Hoover reveled in. He would slouch off to a corner and read market newsletters. But no one criticized him. He was, after all, a financial genius.

Nancy Hoover had found the man of her dreams, the man who could make both of her dreams come true. She was living the high life and showering money on local charities. It was all she had ever wanted.

But a few people were wondering. "It seemed they were trying to accomplish in a handful of years what it takes other families three generations," says Sandra Kritzik.

2

The Royal Couple and Their Subjects

When Nancy Hoover divorced George Hoover to take up with Dominelli, those who knew her "thought she was nuts," recalls a friend.

But soon, the Odd Couple was proving its critics wrong. "They were the perfect Ms. Outside and Mr. Inside. They projected the image most companies try to project," says a San Diego criminal attorney. Most companies would like to have a studious Alexander Graham Bell on the inside putting their product together and a Phineas T. Barnum on the outside selling it. The genius and the genial—the ideal.

Few companies ever achieve this perfect balance, but Dominelli and Hoover seemed to be Bell and Barnum incarnate. They were with each other twenty-four hours a day, starting work at 5:00 A.M. and often toiling through the dinner hour. She sparked the sales effort and served as office manager. He was the "genius" making the pile grow.

By mid-1981 Mr. Inside and Ms. Outside needed a larger staff. And Mark Robert Yarry, the author of the book about commodities—the first to call Dominelli a genius in print— needed a job. "One day I came in, and there was Yarry, working at one of the quote machines," recalls a former employee. Urbane, gregarious, and articulate, the slight (140-pound) Yarry moved quickly. For three months he was a consultant, but soon he was on the permanent payroll.

According to the J. David biography, "Mark Yarry was born in New York City [in 1940]. A graduate of Trinity College, Kentucky, Mark Yarry was a co-founder—along with Gilbert Kaplan and Jerry Goodman (Adam Smith)— of *Institutional Investor*, one of the nation's leading business magazines. A President of the New Orleans Commodities Exchange, he spent several years in England, where he was associated with Arthur Lippert & Co. While in England, Mr. Yarry played a key role in assisting Scotland Yard in breaking up the largest forgery ring in English history. From this experience he wrote a book entitled, 'Fiver!' He is also the author of 'The Fastest Game in Town: Commodities,' which was critically acclaimed."

All that was a little less than half right. There is no Trinity College in Kentucky and never has been, according to the Kentucky Council of Higher Education. (Astutely cognizant of the difference between perjuring oneself in official testimony and puffing oneself in print, Yarry would later— in March 1984—take the Fifth Amendment on whether he had graduated from Trinity. In fact, he took the Fifth Amendment about all his post-high school activities.) Yarry had been the first advertising manager of *Institutional Investor*, "but it's an exaggeration to say he was a cofounder. He was the marketing guy," says current editor Peter Landau.

Nor was Yarry ever president of the New Orleans Commodities Exchange, now the Chicago Rice and Cotton Exchange. Robert Wright, the Lafayette, Louisiana, lawyer who founded the exchange, hired Yarry to sell memberships in the late 1970s. "He was never president. He was talented, but I wondered about him. We parted company by mutual agreement, and as I recall, I was glad to see it happen. It just seemed that one month he would spend $5,000 or $7,000, when I thought he should spend $4,000." "The exchange opened April 9, 1981, and Mark Yarry had been gone for two or three years then," says Leonard Brockman, current president of the exchange. "It's important that the exchange be divorced from him. He was not instrumental in establishing it."

"The stories he told were fantastic," according to Wright's wife, Gay. Yarry said he had been an airline pilot, a concert pianist, a balloonist, a financial adviser to the Rockefellers. The Wrights rented him an apartment and were always puzzled by the many burned candles throughout the rooms. "He was very chauvinistic, very cavalier, strictly weird. He was a very clever, very manipulative kind of guy," says Gay Wright.

Dominelli believed Yarry had a future. He certainly had a past. According to FBI records, while still in his twenties, Yarry had been convicted of practicing medicine without a license and of carrying a concealed weapon. He had attempted to take the California State Medical Boards without benefit of a college degree, much less a medical degree. When denied the opportunity, he complained about the bureaucracy's hidebound ways.

Yarry showed up in London in the mid-1970s and, by all accounts, *did* help Scotland Yard run down a counterfeiter. The experience provided him with material for *Fiver!* and cocktail monologue that would serve him for years. "I had heard that Scotland Yard story so many times. At one party I asked a lieutenant from Scotland Yard if it was true. I was amazed when he said it was," recalls a woman who was Yarry's neighbor at the time.

Hank Whittemore wrote a book, *Find the Magician!*, about the smashing of the counterfeiting ring, and Yarry was one of the book's heroes. Yarry told Whittemore, "I've always lived the good life. I really think I was born two hundred years late. If I'd lived in the eighteenth century, I probably would have been considered a gentlemanly rogue." While in London Yarry first sold eyeglasses out of his basement. Then he moved on to bigger game: diamonds. One day, "he came and asked me if I liked diamonds. Then he pulled a handful out of his jeans pocket. He said he was importing stones," remembers his former neighbor.

Yarry was indeed importing stones—from a Scottsdale, Arizona firm that had named itself "DeBeers," because the South African cartel that controls the diamond trade, De Beers Consolidated Mines Ltd., had not registered the name in the U.S. Yarry was the U.K. representative for the Scottsdale "DeBeers"—but the genuine De Beers was registered, and revered, in Great Britain. The South African firm ran ads disclaiming any connection with the Scottsdale firm and took legal steps to get an injunction. Yarry blithely told *The Times* of London that his company's adoption of the De Beers name was just clever marketing.

Back in the U.S., the founder of the Scottsdale firm was convicted on eight counts of selling low-quality gemstones at inflated prices. At least fifteen thousand people were said to have lost $30 million in the scam. (Yarry was not charged, nor was he a witness, in the case.)

With conditions less than hospitable in Britain, Yarry returned to the U.S. in the late 1970s, peddling memberships for the New Orleans exchange and writing his book on commodities. Then he moved to San Diego and opened a commodities account at the La Jolla Bache office. He lost his shirt trading foreign currencies, but he found a soulmate in Jerry Dominelli.

"Before Yarry got there, Hoover had run the goddamned company," says a salesman who was in on the early days of J. David. But Yarry had his eyes on the throne room.

"At first when I went there, Yarry would be in Dominelli's office eight out of ten times. Later it was nine of ten times. And Dominelli was often in Yarry's office," another former salesman for the firm notes.

Before long, the Odd Couple was the Odd Trio: Dominelli, Hoover, and Yarry.

The J. David strategy soon changed completely. From the firm's founding, Dominelli had recruited investors to put money in pools and partnerships. He would then invest that money in a variety of financial futures contracts and foreign currencies, almost entirely on domestic exchanges that are *regulated*. By law Dominelli had to keep the customers' funds rigidly segregated from corporate funds and from his personal funds. He also had to submit detailed reports of his activities to the Commodity Futures

Trading Commission (CFTC), a federal government agency.

Such requirements didn't sit well with Dominelli, "one of those Chicago people that distrust government . . . a Libertarian like they have at the University of Chicago," as a former employee characterizes him. Dominelli resented making out reports for the government, and he didn't like anyone telling him that he wasn't supposed to mingle customers' money with personal money. His own accountants were never permitted to see the books of his most important operation, the commodity and foreign currency pools and partnerships.

In 1981 an accountant became suspicious that Dominelli was not segregating customer accounts and gave him a warning. Then the CFTC came through to check his books. And the California Department of Corporations started snooping around too, asking if he was selling securities that should be registered with the state.

A friend casually told Dominelli that smart operators could evade the regulators by buying Caribbean "banks." These are not banks at all, of course, but simply plaques in a lawyer's office in a tax-haven country—mail drops, sometimes equipped with a telex machine. They're often called "shell" banks. Entrepreneurs of all descriptions use them to hide ill-gotten gains, to launder drug money, and to dodge domestic regulation. Dominelli reasoned that he might stay out of the regulators' sniffing range by "moving his operation offshore," as lawyers and accountants say.

Generally, there is absolutely no "moving" involved in such an operation. It is accomplished by the flick of an accountant's pencil—making a book entry, the day before the regulator comes, to indicate that the assets are offshore.

In mid-1981 Dominelli paid $40,000 for an offshore

"bank" on the tiny British West Indies island of Montserrat and found an accounting firm willing to issue an audit opinion while abiding by Montserrat's banking statutes, which prohibit anyone from making an audit of funds "moved" there. That temporarily relieved some of his problems, but he was still selling contracts that were under the purview of the CFTC, and the California Department of Corporations still questioned whether his partnerships should be registered.

So Dominelli—greatly influenced by Yarry, according to numerous insiders—then plotted the final getaway. Instead of buying and selling U.S.-registered commodities, he would buy and sell currencies in the foreign exchange market, a totally unregulated market operating twenty-four hours a day all around the world. Often called "interbank," this is by far the world's largest market: On some days, more than half a trillion dollars change hands.

By only trading currencies in interbank and pretending that this activity was taking place inside a plaque on a wall in far-off Montserrat, Dominelli believed he could evade regulation entirely on his pools, thus permitting investors, if they chose, to evade taxes.

The Dominelli-Hoover-Yarry triumvirate concocted a long-term plan to shift the assets of the existing regulated pools into one large pool, then shift that pool into interbank. It would require the OK of the investors. During the transition, the assets of the existing pools would be temporarily "moved" offshore for accounting and tax purposes.

The major part of J. David was to be the interbank foreign-currency fund, which would be kept secret. As interbank grew, J. David would diversify into other areas of finance: stock and bond brokerage, venture capital, and the like. These domestic activities would be regulated, but they would be funded, at least initially, through the clandestine, offshore-based foreign currency operation.

Yarry became the managing director of the Montserrat "bank," which was named J. David Banking Company Limited. Quickly Dominelli's interbank pool was aggressively—and not very subtly—marketed as a tax dodge.

At the end of each year, investors would receive the following missive:

Dear ——:

You will now have received your year-end statement from J. David Banking Company.

In accordance with the policy of the bank, we must advise you that you may have incurred tax liability in the country of your residence and/or nationality.

Under laws of Montserrat, we do not and cannot provide information on your account to anyone outside the jurisdiction of Montserrat and only under highly special circumstances to Montserrat without your consent.

We advise [that] you seek appropriate tax counsel should you believe tax may be due, or deductions allowed on your account.

On behalf of the Board of Directors
J. DAVID BANKING COMPANY LIMITED

It would be difficult to miss the sales pitch in such a message, and word soon got around about the advantages of J. David. Talk increased when, as Dominelli set up additional foreign-currency trading accounts and shifted existing pools to interbank, investors started getting monthly statements informing them of fantastic returns—3 and 4 and 5 percent a month, every month. The statements contained no other information: There was no "paper trail." Investors were not told whether they had bought or sold a certain currency on a particular date, and there were no confirmations of trades made in the investors' names. Nor were Dominelli's interbank accounts audited. Investors were merely informed that their account was up X percent during the month.

Sophisticated investors asked questions. Normally, people get confirmations of trades they make in foreign currency markets. And savvy investors want to know what trades have been made in their behalf and when—and they want the information audited.

"But Dominelli said that if you wanted an audited record, you had to go to somebody else. He claimed he wasn't going to provide that information because people could figure out his secret for making such excellent returns in interbank," recalls an investor.

For the sophisticated investors, it was a battle between common sense and greed, and the latter won. Many had nagging reservations, but the returns were terrific; and best of all, the IRS didn't know. Besides, Dominelli was remunerated only if he made profits for his clients. For his fee he took 20 percent of those profits.

Dominelli's sales force was ecstatic. In the words of one salesman, "We had a product that sold itself."

That was perhaps excessive modesty. J. David's interbank operation sported a polished, hard-driving sales team. At the top was lanky Edward "Ted" Pulaski, a smooth-talking lawyer and ex–Marine officer who had joined J. David after his real estate partnership went bankrupt. Dominelli bailed out the partners financially, helping them meet the payments on their sublet offices—and Pulaski reciprocated by putting his family into J. David investments. The funds came to almost $2 million. Under Pulaski in the sales force were Robert Smith, a former member of an elite Navy team, and John Brockington, a former running back for Ohio State University and the Green Bay Packers. There was an especially aggressive sales force in Orange County. And salespeople in other J. David divisions would direct clients to interbank as well.

"This is inside stuff!" Pulaski would whisper to his potential clients. If they had enough money, he would dispatch a company plane to squire the prospect to La Jolla.

"Pulaski made preposterous claims. 'If you buy, the Holy Ghost will make sure you never go to Hell.' That's the kind of thing he'd tell prospects," snorts a former cosalesman. "Pulaski oversold, but he believed everything he said," says Robert Mengar, one of Dominelli's commodity trading advisers. Pulaski sold interbank to Marine buddies all around the globe.

In a letter Brockington assured prospects that there were "absolutely no liquidity problems. . . . The risks can be limited without sacrificing the profit potential." Investors, he wrote, had "access to a portion or all of their funds within 24 hours notice."

"That letter was questionable," says a former vice-president, "but Brockington was an innocent victim. So was Smith."

Early on, Pulaski realized the promise in wealthy Orange County. After numerous trips he recruited a group of J. David representatives who squeezed the Orange as it had seldom been squeezed before.

Michael Hall, a much-decorated Marine fighter pilot and a Ph.D., headed J. David's Newport Beach office in Orange County. That "Dr." in front of Hall's name added to J. David's aura of respectability. In an interview for a Pepperdine University publication, Hall spoke glowingly of Dominelli's uncanny trading ability. "I think the reason we . . . have grown so quickly is largely because my partner [Dominelli] started trading in foreign currencies at the very beginning of the international money market futures trading, which harks back to 1974," said Hall inaccurately. He claimed that over this nine-year span there was only one loss month, April 1983. (In retrospect it's hard to believe that a university known for its strong business school would let such talk get into print.) According to outside estimates, Hall raised as much as $10 million for J. David.

Dominelli, Hoover, Pulaski, Smith, Brockington, Hall, and the others pushing the program had their own—and their families'—money in the pool. Dominelli was protective of his employees' families' money. Once Pulaski put a relative's money in a pool run by Robert Mengar. Dominelli heard about it and indignantly took it out. "We don't want your family's money in that pool. Put it in my pool where it will be safe," Dominelli said.

The salespeople were paid well for their efforts. Hoover brought home the most—$1.8 million in commissions in just one year—but some of the others, who worked for 0.4 percent commissions per month, earned six figures annually in addition to cars and other emoluments.

Dominelli had recruited the ideal sales force. And just as the he-man types added to the ambience, so did the secretaries. With very few exceptions, they were chosen for their good looks. Dominelli himself would interview secretarial applicants. "The handsome salesmen, the foxes . . . and everybody waiting around to see the guru, Dominelli," remembers Ronald D. Brouillette, a San Diego foreign currency trader who had many occasions to interview Dominelli in his office.

"They were so athletic! So energetic! Their energy made me tired," says an ex-secretary. "The men were so handsome and the women so beautiful. I felt a little out of it, being older. It was like Joe College. People would walk down the halls with a glass of wine in their hands. A lot of the young gals knocked on the guys' doors. I wondered what was going on."

In addition to those on the payroll, there were also the so-called money-finders—individuals outside J. David who were paid commissions to steer their friends, clients, and business associates into the pool. There were lawyers, accountants, business executives, and insurance and real estate salespeople—and at times their commissions reached 20 percent or more annually. It is professionally unethical for accountants and lawyers to accept commissions under such circumstances. Former J. David employees say these professionals were reimbursed under the table—with a car, for example.

The first money-finder was James Kyle, an ex–Marine paratrooper, who was paid 10 percent up front to recruit investors in J. David's beginning months. But Kyle innocently got Dominelli in trouble by distributing his sales brochure outside California. Dominelli was upset. And Kyle, for his part, was getting suspicious of Dominelli. The two severed their business relationship in 1980.

Arthur Axelrod, who had made a fortune in his Anaheim-based salvage business, represented J. David among wealthy Orange County and Palm Springs investors. Axelrod's Transatlantic Bancorp brought in between $10 million and $11 million from movie stars, Southern California real estate salespeople, and others. Including the interest investors believed they were making, Transatlantic eventually had a stake of almost $16 million.

After J. David's downfall, Dominelli complained that Axelrod was charging his customers a double commission. According to Dominelli, Axelrod would give 60 percent of Transatlantic investors' money to J. David, yet would impose a management fee (20 percent of trading profits) on the basis of 100 percent. The remaining 40 percent, Dominelli claimed, was deposited by Axelrod in a Bermuda bank. However, Axelrod's lawyer contends that Axelrod got only half of the 20 percent commission on the 60 percent entrusted to J. David and collected 20 percent of the 40 percent reserve profits, which weren't high. Either way, it was a lucrative setup.

For sheer chutzpah, Reid-Smith Financial got the prize. Proprietress Edith Reid pooled small investors' funds to reach the $50,000 minimum J. David began mandating (with many exceptions) after interbank took off in the 1982–1983 period. Reid took half of what investors made above 20 percent per year; since the annual returns were around 50 percent, she did rather well. (Dominelli claims that she was not paid a commission by J. David.)

Reid had a special plan in which investors could borrow

on the equity in their homes to put money into J. David through Reid-Smith. A physician looked into one partnership based on that principle: There would have been eight investors, and the eighth would have been Reid; but her participation would have been paid by the other seven. "And she was getting a $10,000 commission for putting the deal together," said the doctor, who didn't join. Reid also had "tuition co-ops." Parents of children were encouraged to pull their savings out of their banks and put them in a Reid-Smith pool paying three or four times the bank rate.

Another money-finder, Theron D. Nelsen of Boise, Idaho, had a captive market: distributors of Amway products. Nelsen, a top-level Amway entrepreneur, offered his fellow dealers a combined package: If they put $50,000 into J. David, they would get a guaranteed 2 percent a month. Dominelli, of course, was reporting that investors were making around 4 percent a month, and it is not known what Nelsen did with that other 2 percent.

Nelsen hit up his investors another way: To get in on the action, they had to put an additional $6,000 into Hidden Paradise Ranch, a 4,000-acre cattle ranch and recreational retreat that Nelsen had developed.

Asher Schapiro was an insurance marketer with numerous contacts in New York and La Jolla. He, too, made commissions by bringing people to J. David. And Donald Thomas, Orange County operative, raised perhaps $5 million. Some money-finders were receiving a 10 percent finder's fee and 1 percent per month on all the money that stayed in the pool. This came to more than 20 percent.

But not everyone who had the chance bit. Accountant Ed Blitz says he was twice offered 7 percent on any money he steered into J. David. Because of the accountants' code of ethics, he turned down both offers. A prominent La Jolla real estate broker was offered a $100,000 bonus to join up with J. David, "essentially for the client list," she says. In addition, she was offered the equivalent of 30 percent on all funds that stayed in the J. David pool. "I asked them how they could pay the investors 40 percent and me 30 percent," she recalls. She never got an answer.

The interbank strategy had tapped a rich vein. The money was pouring in. Hoover now saw her chance to start reforming the reactionary establishment. She told intimates that she wouldn't run for office anymore. She wanted to be in the back room pulling the strings.

But she needed expert help for the task. She called on the resources of a professional gadfly whose job would be to review the requests for donations and mete out the funds where they would do J. David the most good. Ironically the in-house gift distributor also became one of J. David's champion gift *recipients*, personally raking in more of Dominelli's largesse than the most productive salesmen. He was George Mitrovich, the community relations director.

"I view myself as a rough-edged person. George is an intellectual. He reads everything and knows so many people," explained Dominelli.

Mitrovich is one of the most inveterate name-droppers in Southern California. One winter evening, clad in a garish red-and-green sport coat, he was preening his feathers at a local restaurant.

Asked if he bought the sport coat in deference to the Christmas season, Mitrovich replied matter-of-factly, "Henry adores it."

"Henry?" asked a local politico. "Henry who?"

"Why, Henry Kissinger, of course," said Mitrovich disdainfully, explaining that he had just returned from a trip to Washington.

At cocktail parties of the Beautiful People, Mitrovich would be introduced to a luminary at the door. Within minutes Mitrovich would be introducing that person as "my dear friend."

Mitrovich, a San Diego native, originally wanted to be a minister, but he had been a poor high school student and had dropped out of college. For some unexplained reason, the official J. David biography was accurate on Mitrovich's background. It only claimed he had *attended* Pasadena Nazarene College and the School of Theology at Claremont. After dropping out, he got a job as an advertising salesman and later became a reporter on a small Whittier paper (his only job as a working journalist, although he later considered himself qualified to be a media critic). From Whittier he went into politics. In 1966 he was press aide to the California lieutenant governor. For three months in 1968, he was a press aide to Robert Kennedy. He claims— but some fellow Democrats dispute his account—that he had been given press relations duties in the hospital the night the senator was assassinated. His association with Kennedy is one of Mitrovich's proudest achievements. He still has a huge picture of the senator in his study, along with the old tag identifying him as a Kennedy staff member. "I have always felt that the highest accolade in politics is to be called a Kennedy person," he sniffs.

After Kennedy's death Mitrovich moved to Washington, D.C. He became press secretary to two liberal senators, Charles E. Goodell of New York and Harold E. Hughes of Iowa. (Goodell, although a liberal, was a Republican. Mitrovich agonized and even consulted Ethel Kennedy before taking the job.) "I loved Washington. I like talking about important things with important people. It was my job to know what important was going on and in what homes, offices, and restaurants it was happening," he said.

Although he loved Washington, he returned to San Diego in 1973, where he began attracting a large following of do-gooders, social climbers, and would-be intellectuals—as well as some of the city's brighter liberals. He made no bones about it: His objective was to turn the city around. "This has been a town run by and for the interests of the Republican Party. Deals are made, understandings are reached, for the benefit of the power structure," he declaimed, heaping much of the blame on the Copley family, which runs the two major daily newspapers. Mitrovich would cite a ludicrous canard that the late James Copley refused to show up at parties attended by Democrats.

Mitrovich contended he had important backing. He would inform those around him, "I have been sent by some high-level Democrats who want me to introduce a more sophisticated level of politics to the party here."

He set up the City Club (identified in the J. David biography as "one of America's leading forums") and undertook to bring heavyweight out-of-town speakers to San Diego. But Mitrovich and his City Club were frequently in financial hot water. The City Club, although very successful, was constantly late with its rent and Mitrovich was constantly borrowing money.

Jerry Dominelli needed credibility and Nancy Hoover wanted to turn the reactionary establishment upside down. What better vehicle than George Mitrovich? Besides, said Dominelli, "He was a friend who needed a place. My first contribution was to George to help put out his City Club newsletter and bring speakers here."

Mitrovich set up shop at J. David headquarters in an elegant office across from the Hoover-Dominelli sanctum. With Dominelli's money Mitrovich recruited top speakers for the City Club—Jimmy Carter, Gloria Steinem, Colorado Gov. Richard Lamm, Delaware Sen. Joseph Biden, *Economist* Editor Andrew Knight—and then brought them by to visit J. David. Dominelli paid Mitrovich more than $6,000 a month, provided him with a red Porsche and a black Peugeot, and permitted him and his family to live in a $750,000 Del Mar house rent-free.

"Am I dreaming?" Mitrovich told a J. David colleague at lunch one day. He couldn't believe what he was being paid for the duties he was performing.

Mitrovich was a general columnist and media critic for a local alternative newspaper, *Newsline.* Issue after issue, he waxed obsequious about the famous people he knew in Washington and railed against the conservative San Diego establishment, taking strong moral stands against greed, hypocrisy, and hosts of minor vices. Before long Hoover and Dominelli were providing $350,000 in financial aid to the paper, although Mitrovich says it was against his better judgment.

That Mitrovich built a following as a crusader was remarkable, given the skeletons in his closet. One name he never dropped was that of Dr. Louis Cella, an Orange County physician and a major contributor to the Democratic Party. Upon leaving Washington in 1973, Mitrovich, as usual, was broke. Dr. Cella put him on salary, loaned him money, and helped him obtain housing in San Diego to work for Democratic candidates in 1974.

In 1975 a grand jury began probing Cella, trying to find if Mitrovich and some other Democratic party functionaries had been slipped hundreds of thousands of dollars through Cella's hospitals. Mitrovich turned state's witness against Cella, acknowledging that, at Cella's request, he had submitted a number of phony bills to the doctor for phantom services to the hospitals, such as a "traffic study" and "hospital promotion services." Cella had told him he needed the false invoices for tax purposes.

Cella was convicted on federal charges of conspiracy, tax evasion, and misappropriation of hospital funds. He later pleaded guilty to state charges of grand theft and filing false Medi-Cal claims, and went to jail. Mitrovich got off completely. Explaining the phony bills he had submitted, he opined, "I should have been more sensitive." And he emphasized over and over that he just did not understand the financial chicanery that was going on.

It's hardly surprising that after he joined J. David, he was sometimes called "the sucker fish that attaches itself to sharks."

Mitrovich did quite a job pumping up the company's image. J. David got massive publicity for its funding of local charities. Mitrovich managed to drop Hoover's name in the newspaper on social and political matters and, with some exceptions, helped keep the press away from the business itself. Dominelli's name showed up in the most uncharacteristic places. *The Paris Review*, one of the world's most prestigious literary journals, listed Dominelli as a major supporter, along with William S. Paley, Arlene and Alan Alda, the National Foundation for the Arts, and the Scripps-Howard Foundation.

At the same time, Mitrovich massaged J. David customers. After bringing Andrew Knight to San Diego, Mitrovich wrote this letter to J. David investors:

Dear Client:

Recently we at J. David had the pleasure of hosting Andrew Knight, the most distinguished Editor of the Economist magazine.

All who met Mr. Knight went away deeply impressed with the depth and range of his knowledge, of his great grasp of world affairs.

When apprised that a lead article of Mr. Knight's would appear in the Spring Issue of Foreign Affairs, the single most influential quarterly in America on matters pertaining to the pursuit of foreign policy, I thought it would serve the interest of our clients to have a copy of Mr. Knight's piece.

Thus we ordered from Foreign Affairs special reprints of "Ronald Reagan's Watershed Year?" for the purpose of making it available to a special group of enlightened and concerned citizens, the clients of J. David.

I am therefore pleased to include with this note a copy of Mr. Knight's Foreign Affairs article. I trust you will find it of great interest and that it will stretch the horizons of your understanding, even as it did mine.

Sincerely,
George S. Mitrovich
Director/Public Affairs
J. David & Company

Most importantly, according to insiders, Mitrovich got Hoover's political power play under way, a power play that centered on Roger Hedgecock. When Hoover lived in Del

Mar, she had been a close personal associate of Hedge-cock, an ambitious young politician who was building a coalition from both the left and the right, wooing environ-mentalists with pleas for growth management and pleas-ing conservatives with demands for fiscal restraint. Hedgecock was a moderate Republican and Hoover a fer-vent Democrat. But in 1980 as a delegate to the Demo-cratic convention, Hoover was socially snubbed by Maureen O'Connor, San Diego's most prominent Democrat. Not long after that, Hoover decided she wanted Hedgecock as mayor. After all, he shared many of her liberal views, and they had worked together in Del Mar. And he would be running against O'Connor.

But Hedgecock and Hoover had become estranged after her divorce. Mitrovich was hired to patch up the differ-ences between Nancy Hoover and Hedgecock over her split-up with George Hoover, claims Alfred O'Brien, a former J. David vice-president. Mitrovich told Hedgecock that Hoo-ver was prepared to back him, O'Brien says, although Mi-trovich disputes the account.

Hedgecock began turning up at Hoover-Dominelli par-ties, and according to grand jury charges, Hoover started feeding him money. His campaign adviser, Thomas She-pard, moved his operation into the J. David headquarters, and Shepard's employees were soon on Dominelli's pay-roll. The newspaper financed by Dominelli and Hoover, *Newsline,* became Hedgecock's most visible supporter.

And Mitrovich became one of Hedgecock's inside advis-ers. They fit together nicely. At an earlier City Club–spon-sored forum, Hedgecock said a "small town psychology" engendered by the rich families whose opinions were set

44

in stone in the 1950s and 1960s had created a crisis in San Diego. Hedgecock, Mitrovich, and Hoover all kept hammering at that theme.

J. David surely benefited financially from its association with liberal Democrats and the Hedgecock wing of San Diego Republicans. Prominent politicians and judges started putting money into the J. David foreign currency fund. Hedgecock was one of them. But more significantly, perhaps, the antiestablishment elitism set the entire J. David organization apart from the rest of the investment community. "To get into J. David, you almost had to have a uniform on," says Michael Aguirre, a San Diego lawyer. "They ate quiche and sipped fine wine and went to the most exclusive restaurants. It was like a sacred rite." Thus did J. David develop a shell that would be very hard to crack.

The cult members enjoyed their private jokes. On December 30, 1982, a seven-page newspaper-style lampoon was distributed to key insiders. The front page banner headline read "Jay Avid Bank Disappears." The text related how "disgruntled investors" complained upon hearing "the news of the bank disappearance." At the time it all seemed very funny.

"They were like the Wizard of Oz," remembers a former employee. The company appeared invincible. Few knew that behind the scenes, the inner circle was a thoroughly undistinguished group: Dominelli; Hoover; Yarry; John Monte, Dominelli's gun-carrying bodyguard; Parin Columna, a handyman; Jerry Russell, a trader-gofer; and Ken Holm, Nancy Hoover's troubled brother. (A few years earlier, Holm had been fired by a local bond brokerage firm for engaging in questionable transactions, and he was financially supported by his sister.) Outsiders, however, primarily saw Hoover, Dominelli, Mitrovich, and the warrior-salesmen.

J. David became the hottest success story in town. Both Mitrovich and Hedgecock called it a great stroke of fate. Hoover and Dominelli represented the business leaders of the future, said Hedgecock.

"J. David & Company has established a remarkable reputation here in San Diego for both its financial success and also for its extraordinary commitment to the betterment of our community. Within the scope of my experience as a public official, I have never known of any company whose sense of community involvement and commitment equals that of J. David," read a letter sent in 1983 by Hedgecock, who by then had become mayor, in support of Dominelli's attempt to obtain a seat on a key London financial board. "To my knowledge, Mr. J. David Dominelli is a person of integrity, community commitment, and has demonstrated a keen understanding of the financial world. Under his able leadership, there has been formed in J. David and its constituent companies, a remarkable success record in a very short period of time." Actually, Mitrovich wrote the letter, but Hedgecock signed it and mailed it under his own name, much to his later chagrin.

If anybody deserved to get rich, Captain Money and the Golden Girl did, said Mitrovich. Look what they were doing to spread their wealth!

3

Prodigality Plus Incompetence Equals Chaos

In early 1982 J. David's accountant approached Nancy Hoover about one of the many inadequacies within the operation.

"The trouble with you is that you make your decisions logically. We make ours emotionally. We're here to have fun," Hoover said, pithily summarizing J. David's modus operandi.

There has never been a more disorderly house than J. David.

Captain Money and the Golden Girl had no knowledge of accounting, bookkeeping, or basic business procedure. "When I asked Jerry about long-range planning, he just laughed at me," recalls a former accountant.

"You'd go to Jerry on an expenditure. He'd say, 'Ask Nancy.' She'd say she'd get back to you. She wouldn't," says another former accountant.

Decisions were based on friendship and emotion. There is no record in Hoover-Dominelliana of any decision made analytically. In his business deals Dominelli considered whether he liked his partner or whether the relationship could lead to more money for his interbank fund or more social prestige for Hoover. The same was true with his loans: The money went to friends and investors in his enterprises, or people Hoover wanted to court. They didn't study the business aspects of any deal, and there is little evidence that they would have known how to do so.

One time, a group of locally prominent entrepreneurs approached Dominelli and Hoover with details of a deal. The J. David pair called in their chief numbers man and asked him to prepare a report. He worked three straight days and nights, finally coming up with solid reasons to turn down the offer. He went to Hoover with his rationale. "Oh, we've already decided to go into that deal," she said breezily. "We don't go by the numbers. We go by the heart."

When Dominelli bought merchandise or contracted for services, he invariably paid far too much. When he entered a business deal, he frequently got taken to the cleaners. When he loaned money, he got fleeced by his own debtors.

The money came in and the money went out, and no one kept track of it. "Jerry had no idea of accounting. He was confused when told things had to add up," says Robert Mengar.

That was particularly true of the checkbook. In fact, a rash of bounced checks eventually brought Dominelli down. However, his checks had been bouncing long before the demise. When the company closed down a money-draining Las Vegas office in 1981, several checks were returned for insufficient funds. Throughout a long relationship with a race car driver, one of every ten of Dominelli's checks proved no good.

Alert investors often became aware of the incompetence. In 1983 an accounting firm asked J. David investors, in a form letter, if they had any observations about the firm. Wrote La Jolla's Robert O'Neill: "J. David & Co.'s management team was in such disarray during the June–August 1983 period that I lost total confidence in any of their accounting procedures. I did not receive account receipts, important account letters, and [I got] inadequate telephone answers from account manager, Jerry Russell, during the above-mentioned period. In short, I would require greater CPA skills than I presently |have] to justify the enclosed statement's accuracy. I must refer your question to the regulating commission for such activities."

Officers of J. David's accounting firm Laventhol & Horwath commented in internal memos about their client's laxity and ineptitude. Eric C. Johnson, a Laventhol tax specialist who was plotting the delicate steps required to keep J. David's Montserrat "bank" free of U.S. taxation, informed the head of the San Diego Laventhol office in May 1983: "We [J. David Banking] can avoid taxation if the people at J. David are willing to cooperate and follow the instructions we give them. However, I don't put a lot of faith in them following through." (Johnson, who later left Laventhol to go with J. David, was wrong; J. David never did pay any U.S. taxes on its offshore tax-haven "bank.")

"On one wall was malfeasance and on the other wall was ineptitude, and in between was total chaos," says one of J. David's first employees.

That was an understatement. Early in the game, this official had resigned when he saw the money Hoover and Dominelli were pouring into their corporate headquarters. "Even if they were making 40 or 50 percent on their money, as they claimed, they were headed for bankruptcy," he said in 1982.

J. David didn't suffer for long in the dank little office beneath the Mexican restaurant. After Hoover resigned from Bache in early 1981 to go with Dominelli's firm full-time, she declared she wanted lavish offices. Dominelli, as always, complied. J. David immediately leased space across the street in a fancy office building, "and then spent $1 million refurbishing it. I told them for that $1 million, they could have *bought* a goddamned building. They were building a fool's empire," says one of the original employees.

At the leased building in downtown La Jolla, "money was no object," recalls Mengar. There were thick carpets, expensive antiques and artwork, costly furniture.

"I was given a brand-new, expensive three-color rug. It hadn't been on the floor two days when Dominelli came in and said, 'It looks like fuckin' Neapolitan ice cream.' He took it out and put down a chocolate rug. But two weeks later, he decided to make the room into a trading room. So he had the chocolate carpet ripped out and he put down fancy parquet-wood floors," says Mengar.

As the company expanded, Dominelli and Hoover decided they needed their own snug retreat. Although they had sunk $1 million into the leased building, they purchased a building next door for almost $2 million. They pumped $500,000 more into it. (After the company's collapse, it sold for just $1.6 million.)

J. David's headquarters were located on the second floor. The main office was Dominelli and Hoover's, with Mitrovich and Yarry occupying nearby offices.

The building "was the plushest office I have ever seen. It was strictly an ego trip, one overimprovement after another," says a real estate appraiser. The building had custom-designed wood floors and ceilings and accordion window shutters of mahogany, and had been, according to the appraiser, "remodeled to resemble the Hearst Castle." There was a private elevator in the front and a private exit in the rear, so that Dominelli could scoot out the door and jump into one of his sports cars undetected. There was a $60,000 generator in the basement, in case the computers went out; and there was a special computer room, although computer usage by J. David was quite unsophisticated. There was a library. And a private kitchen. There were expensive antiques and art pieces on the walls. And a poster of a 1955 Swedish bicycle race, in which all the female participants were pedaling in the nude. There was a private bath with shower, adorned with gold-plated fixtures. In his office Dominelli had a glass jar filled with $50,000 worth of rare coins. An enormous deck surrounded the second floor; the brass would regularly dine there on catered food. And there was an extremely expensive, state-of-the-art electronic security system, replete with electronic beams and motion detectors.

Dominelli had all the latest trading equipment. A Telerate machine, which rented for $800 to $1,000 a month, spewed out all the foreign currency quotations. He had telephones with direct lines to market insiders and also to Wall Street traders, through whom he was supposedly buying and selling currencies. There were Dow Jones and Reuters wires, a telex—"all the glitter," to quote foreign currency trader Ronald Brouillette.

A huge, twelve-foot-high safe was concealed behind wood paneling. Inside the safe were dozens of cash boxes and a tall ladder providing easy access. This was probably the source of the cash that Dominelli always had in his wallet. "Usually, Jerry carried $10,000 in cash with him," says a former executive. "Hoover would also have wads of one-hundred-dollar bills."

Together Dominelli and Hoover would go on shopping excursions. She would stride a few yards ahead of him, pointing to things she wanted. Head bowed, he would shuffle along, pulling out the cash needed for the purchase. "They would breeze through Bullock's. She would point to a piece of furniture she wanted and he would un-roll the bills and pay," says a former employee.

Not surprisingly, they didn't keep track of their purchases. "One of my first days on the job, the accountant asked me if I would call a list of retailers and ask if they would send us invoices for company furniture. He said that the IRS wanted the information, and we didn't have any invoices," remembers a former secretary.

Dutifully she phoned the retailers and requested invoices. "Some of them laughed, but some of them were very nice," she says. "After all, he was a big customer."

Dominelli would routinely pay cash for restaurant meals of more than $1,000, and Sandra Kritzik recalls his buying hundreds of dollars' worth of high-fashion ski clothes for Hoover and paying with cash.

Captain Money opened his wallet to Hoover's children as well, financing cars, expensive trips, and almost anything they requested. He was also generous—but less so—with his own children, who were living with his now-estranged wife.

Dominelli's main love was expensive automobiles. "Jerry was enamored of cars. He bought cars the way a woman buys hats. Whenever he got blue, he'd go buy a $100,000 car," says an ex-employee. The California Department of Vehicles has records on two dozen Dominelli cars, but there were probably around thirty, either registered in other names or perhaps not registered at all. According to a report by the bankruptcy trustee appointed to determine Dominelli's assets after the fall of J. David, there were as many as eighty vehicles under the J. David wing, including Dominelli's cars, those he was giving or selling to others, racing cars, and a fleet of limousines that Hoover purchased. Dominelli was trying to get local permission to build a seventeen-car garage in Rancho Santa Fe and had other vehicles stashed in garages at several locations around San Diego.

Basically it was a recycling arrangement. Paying $50,000 to $100,000 or more each, Dominelli would buy Rolls-Royces, Porsches, Mercedes-Benzes, Jaguars, Alfa Romeos, Ferraris, and Maseratis and drive them for a couple of weeks or months. When he tired of one, he would sell it to an employee or friend at a low price or simply give it away to a productive salesperson or a friend of Hoover's. Then he would buy another.

As in everything else, money was no object. "He once bought a car for $60,000 or $70,000. He told the salesman, 'I'll give you $1,500 more if you have it ready tonight,' " recalls an official probing into J. David's demise.

Dominelli invested $300,000 in La Jolla Ferrari Ltd.,

which had a book value of only $30,000. In return, he would use some of the dealer's luxury cars and avoid paying thousands of dollars in licensing, purchase fees, and taxes. Dominelli called it a "consulting arrangement." After the J. David collapse, La Jolla Ferrari, which had not disclosed Dominelli's investment to the state, was billed for $5,000 in back auto taxes and penalties.

Mark Yarry had a gull-wing Mercedes worth $120,000. Nancy Hoover had a platinum Porsche 911 Targa she kept only two months. Later she got a Porsche 928 convertible, "but didn't like it because it mussed her hair up," says a former employee. Dominelli had a metallic black Porsche 928 that eventually went to one of the subalterns.

Once Dominelli bought a Chevrolet Camaro—an American car. "He had paid $15,000 for it in one-hundred-dollar bills," remembers an ex-employee. Dominelli went to the airport to pick up Hoover. She was livid. "I'm not going to ride in that thing!" she snarled. "The next day," says the former employee, "Nancy Hoover gave [the Camaro] to me, almost to spite Jerry. I had been in the process of trying to lease a car through the company, and she handed me the keys to the Camaro and said, 'Here, take this.' That's the way they gave things away. They almost forced them on you."

Hoover's largesse was not always meant to gain employee loyalty. The husband of a secretary totaled the family car. "Nancy bought her a new VW Rabbit and gave her the pink slip to the car with her name on it. Nancy did things like that with everybody. It was her way," recalls a former secretary.

Hoover and Dominelli had seventeen pieces of real estate around the West, mainly financed with debt. When they started the company, Dominelli lived in an upper-middle-class home in the inland planned community of Rancho Bernardo, and Hoover lived in Del Mar. As they prospered, they moved to the lushest area, Rancho Santa Fe. There they owned a huge $2.2 million estate, as well as two lots worth half a million dollars. The couple had more than $1 million in ski condominiums in Utah, an $800,000 house in La Jolla that was offered to employees rent-free, the $750,000 home used by Mitrovich gratis, and various real estate properties in the San Diego area.

Hoover bought a restaurant in Del Mar and changed its name to Vittorio's (after Dominelli's father). Nightly, Dominelli and Hoover held court at Vittorio's, entertaining customers, receiving those asking for charitable donations, and basking in the attention they received from the oglers.

Dominelli leapt into real estate deals with the slimmest of information, usually supplied by a colleague. In an official examination after J. David's collapse, Dominelli explained to the bankruptcy trustee's lawyers how he got into a project known as Beech Tower Condominiums in San Diego. According to Dominelli, Orange County interbank salesman Mike Hall told him, "I would be doing him a favor in helping him out. He was—obviously couldn't get the place sold, and he was having some problems with the bank on the financing that he had had for the projects, and was now trying to—he had asked his various friends and so forth to purchase places over there, and I guess he had gotten four or five friends to buy condominiums, or at least go on record as buying them or whatever. I don't know." Dominelli made a visit to the condos with Hall, who assured him he would be paying the market price. He snatched up the deal without doing any homework.

Mike Hall was also a partner in a luxury boat Dominelli bought into. In the examination Dominelli was even vaguer on that one: "Essentially there were three partners that owned the boat, and we all—there are papers on it and so forth, which I signed, you know, and so I can't tell you too much about it other than the fact I'm one of the owners of it, and I guess they keep it down in—I believe it's St. Vincent or St. Thomas."

Dominelli had earlier told others that he didn't particularly like boats. But he *did* like airplanes—especially after officials of a Chicago commodities firm, Refco, came to visit him in a private jet. "When he saw Refco's private plane, his eyes just bugged out. He was as excited as a kid buying chocolate," says a former employee. Initially J. David was spending upwards of $50,000 a month flying air taxis. After the Refco visit, Dominelli decided he had to buy a plane. He wound up buying two and leasing a third. First he purchased a Lear 24 jet for $600,000 and got a lease on a Lear 35. But those didn't sate his ego, and in mid-1983 he arranged to buy a 1967 Grumman Gulfstream II for just over $5 million. To do so, he agreed to pay 22 percent interest—a horrendous rate at the time.

Just after that commitment, Chris Kalabokes came in as J. David's chief financial officer. He told Thomas LaHay, senior vice-president of San Diego's First National Bank, J. David's main banker, that Dominelli had paid an "outrageous interest rate on terms that partially handcuffed the company." Dominelli insisted it was "the only way we could get the plane financed at the time." The purchase would turn out to be one of Dominelli's most critical blunders.

J. David's charitable contributions were another un-monitored drain. Almost $200,000 went to the San Diego Symphony, about $100,000 to the San Diego Opera, and about $100,000 to the La Jolla Museum of Contemporary Art. Hoover, reveling in her press coverage, gave large sums to Del Mar institutions. And a third of a million dollars went to the University of California at San Diego for a swimming pool, an arts center, and medical research.

Just before the company went bankrupt, a La Jollan went to see Hoover about a possible gift for a local charity. He asked for $60,000, hoping to get $20,000. "I gave my spiel. I sat back, expecting the arguments. There were none. They committed the money—all of it," he remembers. (The charity, though, never got the money.)

"Jerry couldn't say no to a friend," says William Galt, a large investor.

"She wanted to give away money and he couldn't say no," recalls a former top vice-president of the firm. "It was a deadly combination."

Almost $60,000 went to KPBS, the local public-broad-casting radio and television affiliate. One of the best-pub-licized events, partly funded by J. David money, was a televised debate among the U.S. Senate Republican primary candidates in spring 1982. The City Club, sponsor of the debate, was trying to shake the perception that it was only a Democratic forum. The local media gave the debate extensive play, and Mitrovich, of course, raved on and on about it in his *Newsline* column.

But six months later KPBS was still trying to collect from Mitrovich. Gloria Penner, a popular local TV personality, had written several letters to Mitrovich. On November 10,

Eldon H. Hale, the station's administration manager, wrote, "For five months KPBS has been attempting to collect from you the balance due to us for the expenses we incurred in broadcasting the U.S. Senate debate on May 25, 1982. On June 11, 1982, you wrote to Gloria Penner, promising payment upon your return from France. On July 14th, I spoke with you and you promised payment, 'in the next week or so.' Gloria wrote again on August 4th and September 1st. Additionally, there were several telephone conversations and promises made before and since that time, including a 'promise' to bring the payment with you to KPBS on November 3rd. The purpose of this letter is to make a final request for payment in order to avoid further action and the resultant legal expenses for both of us."

On November 16, an indignant Mitrovich wrote Penner on City Club stationery. Two of his City Club supporters had each anted up $500.

My Dear Penner:

Enclosed please find the checks promised. They total $1,000, as promised.

The balance will follow shortly.

Also, and on a less positive note, the phone call from Eldon Hale to Jerry Dominelli, as in J. David Dominelli, wanting to know about the monies owed, was not, repeat, was not, appreciated. Period.

I always said that I would make good the money, not J. David. The $4,000 given by J. David was more than enough. J. David did not need to give more. Moreover, I would not have permitted J. David to have given any additional monies.

This was a City Club obligation, not a J. David obligation. Calling the person I work for was an exercise in very poor judgment. While it is true that the burden of this was on me, one that I assumed, the delay was not altogether my fault. It did take some time for me to receive from KPBS a statement as to why the cost was $2,000. Even then the statement I received was not very precise.

But, to go back to the call from Eldon to Jerry, the more I've thought about it, the more annoyed I've become. The bitter taste will linger a while.

Sincereley [sic],

George Mitrovich
President

Despite such occasional unpleasantness, J. David succeeded in becoming known as one of San Diego's great benefactors. There was an important quid pro quo: People connected with the arts groups were moved to invest heavily in the J. David interbank fund. The sums the arts patrons invested were greater than the monies J. David donated to the institutions.

Dominelli and Hoover also spent millions of dollars supporting athletics. Some $40,000 went to the San Diego Crew Classic. Dominelli made a multithousand-dollar contribution to a local marathon—in cash, the day of the race.

Dominelli, who frequently received speeding tickets, was a fast-car addict. At parties, when he would be huddled in the corner reading a book and those around him would be marveling at his intellectual curiosity and amazing attention span, Dominelli wouldn't always be studying books and newsletters on international investing. Often he would be reading pulp magazines about sports cars.

Dominelli pumped millions of dollars into race car teams. He first backed a San Diegan, Wayne Baker, but in 1982 decided he wanted international prestige. He became the angel for John Fitzpatrick Racing, which competed on European as well as American tracks, such as the nearby Riverside Raceway. At Riverside Dominelli would entertain potential investors and any Beautiful People Hoover was trying to woo. They would sip drinks under a guest tent and would be joined by the race car drivers and mechanics after the event.

Dominelli said he owned 50 percent of the Fitzpatrick team. After the collapse of J. David he told the bankruptcy trustee, "I'd say my part is worth, minimum, three-quarters of a million dollars. The race cars alone are worth anywhere from $200,000 to $250,000. Each spare motor is $50,000." Some think Dominelli poured between $2 million and $4 million into the venture.

It ended abruptly. A driver was killed at one of the races, and the story goes, Hoover couldn't stand any more violence.

Others say that story is apocryphal. What happened, they contend, is that, at the request of his estranged wife, Antje, Dominelli had Fitzpatrick appear as a promotion at a sporting goods store Dominelli had financed for her. "When Hoover found that out, she hit the ceiling. I mean she was throwing things. She gave an ultimatum to Jerry—one of many she gave—and that was the end of racing," says a top official of J. David at the time.

J. David achieved international prominence through its sponsorship of a triathlon team. The triathlon is a grueling event: Participants in the "ultra" event swim 2.4 miles, then bicycle 112 miles and run 26.2 miles. Ted Pulaski, the top salesman, took an active interest in the triathlon and later became the national over-40 champion. Hoover and her two college-age children, Georgie and Nina, were on the team.

In October 1983 *Sports Illustrated* lauded Dominelli as "Triathlon's Sugar Daddy." J. David had its athletes on salaries of $1,000 to $1,500 a month. Team members were provided the finest equipment and stayed in the finest hotels around the world. One of the team members was photographed running along with a wad of bills in his hand. It was to symbolize J. David's largesse in an article for *Triathlon Magazine,* a publication J. David helped finance. Hoover and Dominelli transported the team to events all around the world. Hoover would rent a helicopter to view the races. Over three years J. David put more than a third of a million dollars into the triathlon.

Hoover and Dominelli put much more into horse racing. Since they lived in horsy Rancho Santa Fe, it was perhaps inevitable that they would take up the sport. They formed Hoover Farms, and in 1983 paid more than $650,000 for four horses. (One unnamed yearling had a dam by the name of Takethemoneyandrun.) The horses achieved moderate—extremely moderate—success, and members of the horse-breeding set were reportedly eager to unload more mediocre merchandise on the newcomers to the sport. One of San Diego's most prominent horsemen, astonished by the prices that Dominelli was shelling out for horses, concluded that he must be on cocaine. According to bankruptcy records, Hoover paid $230,000 for a horse that later sold at auction for all of $7,000.

Not surprisingly, Hoover Farms didn't last long. After J.

David's collapse, the ownership of the horses was quietly shifted, and the horses started racing under another stable's name. Hoover Farms has disappeared.

In connection with all their activities—cultural, athletic, business—Dominelli and Hoover threw parties costing thousands of dollars. They feted the triathletes. Their man Mitrovich entertained City Club speakers and other dignitaries. They staged a massive party when their man, Hedgecock, was elected mayor. They held annual Christmas parties for the employees' children.

Hoover could barely talk about anything else. In early 1983 Dominelli had a $400,000 lawsuit pending against the former head of one of his subsidiaries. One Friday afternoon, the plaintiff and defendant and a battery of lawyers hissed and scratched through a tension-filled meeting at J. David headquarters. At its conclusion Hoover suggested they all adjourn to a local drinking spa. Hoover opened the conversation with "Let's plan our next ski vacation."

In fact, several weeks after the company had been thrown into bankruptcy, and Dominelli was being threatened with jail unless he revealed the whereabouts of the investors' money, "Hoover threw a party, and she was talking about having a big beach party in the summer for all the old employees," says a former executive.

Dominelli loaned money to friends—and went into side business deals with them—as casually as he bought sports cars and horses. "He would reach some kind of an agreement and then would send me to do the detail work. But the story at the other end would not be the same story he told me. Then I'd go back to him, and he would be fuzzy on the details," recalls a former accountant with the firm.

George Munger, proprietor of Piret's, a French restaurant numbering Roger Hedgecock among its patrons, came to Hoover and Dominelli for money. "Nancy and I sat there with him, and it wasn't really any big negotiation," Dominelli later told the bankruptcy trustee. "We just agreed, because he needed the money at the time."

The terms of the loan? "It was agreed that he could pay us back almost on any basis he wanted," explained Dominelli. The maturity of the loan? "As soon as he was able to pay us back." The amount of the loan? "I think that we had agreed to loan him as much as—if I'm not mistaken—a hundred thousand dollars. As far as how much we had given him, I think that we had given him about—it was either $50,000 or $75,000. I'm not positive," said Dominelli.

Was the borrower going to pay interest on the loan? The bankruptcy trustee was curious. "I forgot what we had decided on that," replied Dominelli.

Dominelli loaned money to former San Diego Charger football player Speedy Duncan and was equally vague on the specifics. He also loaned money to Yarry and Pulaski for homes. Although Pulaski was making $40,000 a month on commissions, he would constantly run out of money "the second or third week" of the month and come to Dominelli for an advance, according to Dominelli. (Pulaski kept getting behind because he was paying people to bring him customers, Dominelli contended—a story Pulaski denies.)

When examined by the bankruptcy trustee on details of the various loans and investments, Dominelli was generally foggy and forgetful. Even if, as some investigators think and as certainly seems likely, he was coyly covering up bad or shady deals, Hoover's characterization rings true: Captain Money and the Golden Girl *did* make their deals from the heart, rather than on the basis of the numbers. Dominelli's vagueness under examination was only partly Machiavellian.

The same sloppiness was evident in the launching of J. David's subsidiaries. Dominelli had that dream of becoming another Goldman, Sachs—an investment conglomerate offering all kinds of financial products. In the four years the firm operated, J. David had upward of fifty subsidiary operations pushing different kinds of investments. Almost all of them were losing money, although it's doubtful Dominelli knew that. He was told the ancillary operations were a drain, but he didn't try to pare them back until it was too late.

Dominelli purchased some of the operations, such as Teachersworth Services, which sold annuity insurance contracts to teachers. Others were started from scratch. J. David Mercantile Group was a venture capital/syndication subsidiary that financed a startup high-tech firm and was searching for others. Under it was Mercantile Management Company II, which offered limited energy partnerships: J. David Energy I, J. David Energy II, and J. David Energy III.

J. David Intercurrency served as a broker arranging foreign currency transactions between banks. J. David Trading was a commodity trading adviser dealing in regulated commodities. Systematic Risk was a partnership formed to apply modern portfolio theory to the selection of commodity trading advisers. Dominelli and the founder squabbled, and the operation fell away from J. David long before J. David's demise. On its own, it is now prospering.

J. David Natural Resources was Dominelli's piece of a Northern California silica- and gold-mining operation named Yuba Natural Resources. Dominelli was a one-third partner in a group that bought up roughly half of the old-line company. The other partners were prominent in California politics: Richard Silberman, former chief adviser to Gov. Jerry Brown, and M. Larry Lawrence, former chairman of the California Democratic Party. Dominelli tried to resell his piece to his investors, but failed at the task.

One of the biggest drains was J. David Securities, the stock-and-bond marketing operation. Dominelli opened offices in several large cities and recruited brokers by offering commissions that were substantially higher than those they could get at other firms. "I did a study to show him that he would lose money paying those commissions, but he ignored it," says a former accountant. (Many of the stockbrokers also picked up extra commissions, mainly under the table, by steering investors into Dominelli's foreign currency pool.) Dominelli fought hard to keep the subsidiary going.

In the end a consultant informed him that J. David Securities was losing at least $1 million a month, if the salaries and commissions, leasehold improvements, and rentals were properly charged to the operation. According to the consultant, "He paused and said, 'Well, maybe we can turn it into a discount brokerage.' I told him, 'Discount brokerages have linoleum floors and Army surplus desks. You have the most plush offices in the U.S.'"

And there were divers other subsidiaries: Cambier Management; Treasury Life Holding Co. and its underlings, Southwest Industrial Life and Treasury Life Assurance Co.; J. David (Asia); Capital Assets Managers; J. David Municipals and Governments; and on and on.

Dominelli would launch a new venture, or make an acquisition, on a whim: "One time a shark friend of mine called," remembers Robert Mengar. "He said, 'Your man Dominelli is a real mark. A friend of mine called him with a deal [a piece of the equity in a small company]. They talked awhile. Finally, Dominelli offers him about three times the maximum he thought he could receive. About knocked him off his chair.' " The operation he bought eventually became one of the subsidiaries, and like the others, it was insignificant except for the strain it was placing on the company.

Besides the massive losses, the subsidiaries had one thing in common: No one knew how Dominelli was paying for them. "There was this big black hole. Every time you asked where the money was coming from, you couldn't find out. He wouldn't let you know how he was financing them," says one accountant.

"We were never permitted to see where the money was coming from," says another accountant.

"He wrote checks to support the other enterprises. He called it his 'magic checkbook.' Other times he called it his 'slush fund,' " recalls a third accountant.

An employee who inquired where Dominelli was getting the money to fund an offshoot operation was told laughingly, "Dominelli Airlines."

When Dominelli wrote these checks, he often had little idea if he had money in the account to cover them. "One time I was in his office, and he had agreed to support a project of mine. He said he'd write me a check. He had Debra [one of his secretaries] call the bank to find if there was money in the account," says Mengar. Told how much was in the account, Dominelli beamed, "Oh, good. I can write a check on it."

"The source of funds [for J. David Securities] was a matter of conjecture," explains a consultant who often asked himself if clients' money was being used to finance the other operations—and Hoover and Dominelli's spending sprees. "I don't think he [Dominelli] had any understanding of accounting," the consultant goes on. "So much came in every day and so much went out. The money just went into one pool, and no one except those in the inner circle got a glimpse of the pool. The place was run out of a checkbook by someone who didn't know how to balance a checkbook."

Other accountants made the same observation. In an investment operation, client funds must be kept rigidly separate from other funds. But several accountants who worked for J. David wondered whether there was commingling—whether the investors' money was being put into an account with other funds and used for noninvestment purposes, such as paying the bills of a subsidiary or paying for one of Hoover's horses or Dominelli's expensive autos.

"You don't want to believe that your employer is a crook," says an accountant, who became convinced upon discovering that an investor's check had been deposited in a corporate account at Morgan Guaranty in New York. The accountant told Dominelli the practice had to stop, "but he tossed it [the accountant's warning] into that big pile of papers he had. Nancy once asked, 'Why do we need an accounting department? Bache across the street doesn't have an accounting department.' She didn't understand that Bache had three floors of accountants at its New York headquarters. As the French say, it was *folie à deux,* or 'folly of two.' "

This accountant still is not sure whether Hoover "actually understood the difference between client funds and her own funds." Once when a payment was late, Hoover airily explained to a vendor, "Oh, a customer's check bounced."

After only six months with the company, the accountant resigned and informed the FBI of the irregularities at J. David. This accountant was the first—but hardly the last—to go to the FBI.

Many of J. David's follies were actually follies of one: Nancy Hoover. "She ran the company in the administrative sense," recalls a former senior financial officer of J. David. "She determined who was hired. She hired friends, friends of friends, family members, investors, friends of investors. There was no planned growth. She would say, 'Five more people were hired this month, so we need another office.' People came in Monday and found they were reporting to another person. The rank and file was in confusion. People didn't understand what they were supposed to do. In the course of three years, some people were moved ten times."

"The unprofessionalism was unbelievable," according to one investor. "After I decided to remove my money, I called and asked to be sent the interest over the past couple of months. A clerk said, 'Fine,' and that was it. She never asked for my account number. Two days later I called and asked for the $50,000 principal, and she said the same thing, 'Fine,' and never asked me the account number or anything."

Basically, Hoover handled the administration because she was as decisive as Dominelli was indecisive. He relied upon her judgment for all business details, particularly their spending. "Hoover ran the firm. She ran internal policy. She was the fairy princess ruling over her empire, moving desks and personnel around to her preference. People were either on her favored list or unfavored list. People would be elevated and heads would roll according to Nancy's plan, with no rhyme or reason," says an ex-official.

The chaos grew. Finally, Yarry convinced Dominelli that the company needed an office manager to relieve Hoover of some of her administrative burdens and to free her up for the sales duties at which she excelled.

Thus did one Richard Colabella, a former colleague of Yarry's at *Institutional Investor*, join J. David in 1982. "Colabella came in as a hatchet man, but he made the mistake of announcing he was a hatchet man," a former vice-president remembers. "He tried to talk in a gravelly voice like the Godfather and use Italian gestures, but he also wanted people to know how cultured he was."

He fit snugly into the J. David environment. "When I was interviewing for the job, he spent the entire time trying to get a powder blue Cadillac for one of the vice-presidents in Orange County," says a former secretary.

Colabella would frequently throw tantrums that friends say resulted from a stomach disorder. "He would be raging violently, then he would take some of his medicine, and pretty soon he would mellow out," recalls a former employee.

According to several intimates, Hoover resented both Yarry and Colabella. This was one reason that Hoover and Dominelli would frequently get into bitter arguments that rattled the mahogany shutters, damaged morale, and sent visitors scurrying for cover.

"First, they would just be bouncing ideas off each other.

Then their voices would start to rise. Then the door would close . . . and all hell would break loose," remembers a former employee. By some reports, Hoover could match and often one-up Dominelli's profanity.

They feuded primarily about company matters, such as intrusions by Yarry and Colabella. But they also argued about personal matters—most frequently, Dominelli's reluctance to divorce his wife.

"One time, a fellow had been waiting outside their office for two and a half hours," says a former executive. "They started to argue and Nancy started telling Jerry that he was no good in bed and never had been any good in bed. One of the secretaries came to the man and told him that Mr. Dominelli and Mrs. Hoover would not be able to see him that day, and that he should go home.

" 'Are you kidding? I wouldn't miss this for anything,' said the visitor."

At the peak of most donnybrooks, Hoover would bolt out of the office, with Dominelli in pursuit, yelling, "Nan! Nan!"

One former employee even claims to have witnessed physical violence: "I heard these sounds. I heard hollering, screaming, and bad language. I rushed out in the hall. Nancy had picked up Jerry by the throat and she was banging his head against the wall."

As time went on and hostilities escalated, employees increasingly sensed that something was even more wrong than they suspected—that there was pressure on Hoover, Dominelli, Yarry, Colabella, and the others that was almost unendurable.

The in-house cleric, George Mitrovich, tried to serve as peacemaker. He took Colabella to lunch and explained how his outbursts hurt personnel relations. He pleaded with

Hoover and Dominelli to do their fighting outside the office.

"But poor George didn't understand," chuckles a former J. David official.

4

Ponzi Revisited?

Captain Money and the Golden Girl knew nothing about business, about accounting, about planning—but they seemed to be succeeding amazingly well. Though sharply criticized by their colleagues in financial circles, they gloried in the role of revolutionaries breaking new ground on the way to wealth. How better to show up the reactionary establishment they despised?

Dominelli and Hoover were hardly the first to have taken an irregular route to riches. More than sixty years before J. David was defying all the conventions in San Diego, one Charles Ponzi was doing the same in Boston.

Like the officers at J. David, Charles Ponzi had considerable trouble getting his biography straight. For example, he would boast around the bars of Boston that he had attended the University of Rome for three years, but in fact he had little formal education. He also neglected to point out that prior to taking the name Ponzi, he had gone by the names Bianchi and Ponsi. And he never mentioned that he had spent time in a Canadian prison for forging signatures on checks.

Initially, in Boston, Ponzi had a series of low-paying and low-prestige jobs, such as dishwashing and clerking. But he was looking assiduously for an angle, and one day he found one. He gazed at an International Postal Reply Coupon inside a letter he had received from his native Italy.

As John Train, writing in the May–June 1984 *Harvard Magazine,* noted, "The coupon had in fact been bought in Spain. Because International Postal Reply Coupons were redeemable anywhere at fixed rates of exchange negotiated from time to time by the participating governments, while currencies themselves can fluctuate wildly, this coupon had cost Ponzi's correspondent only one-sixth as much to buy in Spain as it was worth in stamps of the United States. Well! Why couldn't you march into the post offices of some benighted land whose currency had collapsed, and acquire stacks—bales, indeed—of these coupons for next to nothing, and thereafter, presenting them for redemption in a strong-currency country, make an immediate, huge profit in stamps? After that, one would need only to wholesale the stamps, perhaps, to business firms at a slight discount. The thing was a gold mine!"

Of course, adds Donald H. Dunn, author of *Ponzi! The Boston Swindler,* the famed Bianchi-Ponsi-Ponzi really didn't intend to go to so much trouble. He would just *tell* his investors that he was doing that with their money.

That's how the term "Ponzi scheme" came into existence. In a Ponzi scheme, investors' money is not invested in anything. The early investors are paid off with money coming in from later investors, and thus the survival of the scam depends on the continuing recruitment of new investors. But with each new investor, the scheme goes further in the hole long-term. The roof has to cave in at some point.

There are thousands of Ponzi schemes going on at any given time all around the world. Recently, the FBI estimated that at least two hundred Ponzis were afoot in Los Angeles alone. Some are pyramid clubs and chain letters. Others are large marketing businesses that depend for their success on selling dealerships in a product, rather than the product itself.

Ponzi was out to prove to the Boston establishment that an outsider could make big money, too. He knew that he had to attract prominent judges, politicians, lawyers, and affluent citizens to his scheme. With the help of a hired public relations man, he did so and gained instant credibility.

It was important to the public relations mystique that Ponzi distribute his wealth to the needy. "Ponzi gave $100,000 to an orphanage," says Dunn. "According to him, he wasn't making money for himself. He was helping poor immigrants—making money to show that an immigrant could come up by his bootstraps."

To impress the public, it was equally important that Ponzi display his wealth. This he did with flair. He moved his wife and mother to a home in the suburbs. He spent liberally and carried wads of cash and checks on his person. He rode around Boston in a chauffeured limousine.

Ponzi recruited a group of agents—money-finders, in essence—to whom he paid a 10 percent finder's fee. They, and Ponzi himself, pounded the pavements of Boston, offering investors 50 percent if they left their money in for forty-five days and 100 percent for ninety days. Exuding confidence, Ponzi put the hard-earned money of his wife, her brother, and her father into his operation, named the Securities Exchange Company. As Bostonians heard of the fantastic returns on their money, eager investors began queuing in front of the Securities Exchange office.

Ponzi said he was investing the money in International Postal Reply Coupons, but in fact he spent it on himself, his home, and his lush lifestyle—and on various enterprises.

Flush with cash, Ponzi acquired one-fourth of an establishment bank by putting several million dollars in it (at 5 percent interest), then threatening to withdraw the money unless he got his way. He took over an export-import company where he had once been a lowly clerk. He dreamed of buying the mothballed World War I fleet and starting a world shipping operation.

In Boston Ponzi was hailed as a financial genius. But inside his company, everything was chaos. He kept no books in the conventional sense. He just kept notes, scribbled on pieces of paper, promising to pay people X amount after X amount of time. "Six clerks stacked piles of banknotes in closets until they scraped the ceiling. Wastebaskets did duty as coffers for greenbacks," says Train.

When questioned about his scheme, Ponzi refused to give many specifics: He didn't want people to learn his secrets, he explained.

The state government got very interested, and Ponzi shifted the onus to it: If it would let him stay open, investors would get their money, he insisted. But if it shut him down, they wouldn't.

"Ponzi really believed that everybody would get paid back—he just knew that they couldn't possibly get it back all at once. Therefore, he blamed it all on the government," says Dunn.

The accountants called in by the government were thoroughly confused. They were accustomed to balance sheets and profit-and-loss statements, and Ponzi's piles of IOUs threw them for a loop. So did Ponzi: He took great joy in confusing the head accountant every chance he could.

Such behavior is typical of the con artist: He gets his kicks by concocting a new lie at every turn in the road. It's exhilarating to come up with new creative explanations for every dilemma. "With $10 million, you can buy judges, you can buy time, you can buy lawyers—you stall, you stall, hoping something will come along," explains Dunn. He adds, "Everything Ponzi said was a lie."

The bona fide con man stays cool in the heat of every crisis. His serenity reassures investors, who decide to keep their money in the pot despite their reservations. The con man keeps his cool because he is, in fact, somewhat detached from reality. He can't understand what he has done wrong, because he can't fully distinguish right from wrong. He *believes* in his scheme; it has made him rich, and he won't abandon it now.

Ponzi was perfect in that role. After the press started snooping around, long lines of angry investors demanded their money be returned. But the cool, still-cocky Ponzi assuaged the people, pointing out that everyone who asked for his money was getting it back. A certified check for a million dollars sat in open view in Ponzi's pocket. Convinced, many left their money in, just as Ponzi had planned.

However, Ponzi's public relations man deserted him, and the press started breathing more heavily down Ponzi's back.

More lines appeared. Ponzi claimed the establishment bankers and establishment press were persecuting him. He filed a $5 million libel suit against one of the papers. But the Massachusetts State Banking Commission closed down Ponzi's lead bank, and one newspaper revealed that he had spent time in jail in Canada. Finally, the auditors figured it all out: The old investors were simply being paid off with funds from new investors. Ponzi was $3 million short.

He was charged with mail fraud, conspiracy, and grand larceny. Civil suits piled up. He had little money left, so he served as his own lawyer part of the time. But Bostonians cheered him as he was escorted to court. After all, he had made many of the early investors rich.

Despite his obvious guilt, he never left town. "He really believed he could continue outsmarting the authorities. He had done it before—there was no reason he couldn't continue doing it," says Dunn. "It takes a certain kind of genius to escape with the money. But Ponzi thought he could pull it off."

Ponzi went to jail once again, still believing in his scheme. He promised to pay the investors back—and many had faith in him, even after he got out of prison, jumped bail, and wound up in Florida selling lots that were under water, offering investors 200 percent profits in sixty days. He landed in jail again and eventually was deported to Italy, still assuring investors that he would pay them in full.

Reportedly, he became a pilot for Mussolini, then went to South America, where he got involved in the diamond and emerald trade. He died in a charity hospital, writing his memoirs and still promising to pay investors back.

———

From J. David's beginning in 1979, prominent San Diegans—and Dominelli's colleagues in the brokerage business—suspected he was running a Ponzi scheme.

"Because Dominelli had been so unsuccessful in business, we thought there was a Ponzi scheme going, perhaps also in connection with a money-laundering operation," says the manager of one of the largest brokerage offices in La Jolla, located very near Dominelli's headquarters.

For one thing, Dominelli's widely distributed eye-popping track record didn't square with his observable investment performance. One of his first money-finders, for example, asked Dominelli to set up a foreign exchange account at Clayton Brokerage in St. Louis. The money-finder wanted to test Dominelli's track record there against what he was telling investors they were receiving. "He was losing in the St. Louis account, but claimed to be making money for his clients," says the money-finder. Suspicious, he checked with professionals in the interbank market. "People in the interbank market said they never saw the opposite side of the trade—they never saw the J. David name appear [in buying and selling records]," continues the money-finder, who ended his relationship with J. David in the spring of 1980.

In 1979, while starting J. David, Dominelli had set up a personal commodities account at Drexel Burnham Lambert. He was trading currencies, metals, and interest rate futures through a broker, Jon Strebler. Dominelli began with $20,000 to $30,000, according to Strebler, and right along, "he was losing his ass." Because he was trading on borrowed money, Dominelli had to add amounts of $10,000 and $20,000—probably putting in as much as $100,000 as margin calls mounted, adds Strebler. And he was losing steadily.

Strebler checked Dominelli's actual trading performance against the published track record. "Perhaps as many as 50 percent [of his actual trades] did not match with his track record," says Strebler. He suspected that Dominelli's published track record omitted losing trades. Strebler regarded it as "inaccurate and misleading to show a track record which only reflected some of Mr. Dominelli's trades of a specified period.

"I alerted my fellow brokers at Drexel, and anyone else who asked me about Mr. Dominelli's trading, and anyone else who I even thought might be considering turning money over to him, about the discrepancies in track records, and about my lingering doubts about his trading results," says Strebler.

Bache came to have similar doubts. Early in J. David's existence, Dominelli did his trading through Hoover, who was still at Bache. But John Farrish, the manager, became increasingly wary of Dominelli and also irked that he was hiring some of his Bache salespeople.

In June 1982 Farrish wrote to Dominelli. "I've received numerous requests for verification of your past trading record," read the letter. Dominelli had been telling clients that in one Bache account he had made $28,064. "In checking our records for this account, we show a cumulative loss of $28,315," the letter noted. Similarly, Dominelli claimed that he had made $15,764 in another account, but, wrote Farrish, "Our records show a cumulative loss of $2,037. . . . Since I assume we will continue to get inquiries, I would appreciate your advice on where the discrepancy lies in our numbers." Dominelli never replied.

"When people would ask me, I would tell them that I would not recommend that people put accounts with him for several reasons. One is that clients did not get confirmations of trades. Secondly, I hadn't seen any verified record to prove that he could make the kind of returns that he was promoting that he was making," says Farrish.

Dominelli's first manager at Bache was William Taylor, who later moved over to Drexel, where he would occasionally field inquiries about Dominelli. "When Jerry started publishing his track record at Bache, I was asked, 'Is it really true?' I gave [the inquiries] to John Farrish. I never saw the documentation, but from all the feedback I got, I understood that it was not true," recalls Taylor.

When Dominelli asked the La Jolla office of Drexel to clear transactions for him, Taylor set the cash deposit so high that Dominelli went elsewhere.

After he stopped trading through Bache, however, Dominelli did trade for a period through the New York office of Drexel. That arrangement lasted only a short time, and Dominelli then moved his small account to Merrill Lynch, Wall Street's largest firm.

Dominelli told Merrill Lynch that the account was his own money, not that of his customers, according to George Bullette, senior resident vice-president of Merrill Lynch in San Diego. "The account was not successful. We were not comfortable with it," Bullette says. "Because of the losses, we asked that the account be closed." There had been a number of margin calls.

But it wasn't just the losses bothering Merrill Lynch.

Through the years, it had heard conflicting stories from Dominelli. He told one high Merrill Lynch official that his wife had a good deal of money. But he also had told a top official of J. David that somebody outside, whom he wouldn't identify, was backing the firm to the tune of $400 million. Such stories got around. Merrill Lynch's La Jolla organization, located in the same building as J. David, gave the company a negative report.

From its New York headquarters, Merrill Lynch checked out Dominelli through Interpol, the computerized international police operation, according to a source in the firm. The Interpol report was negative, says this informant. (Officially, Merrill Lynch won't discuss the matter.) In any event, Merrill Lynch closed Dominelli's interbank account in early 1983, citing large losses. Later, Dominelli was to claim that Merrill Lynch closed the account because it believed that Mark Yarry had organized crime connections. Merrill Lynch refuses to talk about that aspect.

Without Merrill Lynch, Dominelli had almost no access to the interbank market. J. David continued to report fat profits to the investors each month, but there was only a small amount of trading done through two European banks. In fact, *throughout* J. David's existence, the trading Dominelli did was very small in relation to the money that investors were handing him. "The actual trading was just peppercorns," to quote a former sales executive.

Dominelli had lost heavily in every foreign currency account people had knowledge of: at Bache, Drexel, Merrill Lynch, Clayton Brokerage, and in a small mutual fund of currencies that Dominelli had purchased. The value of the fund—based on the English Channel island of Guernsey—plunged 23 percent after Dominelli bought it. But investors did not find out about these losses until after J. David's collapse. Then it was clear that Dominelli's track record had been a complete fabrication. "He was like the tout at the racetrack who buys a ticket on every horse. One of them wins, and he shows people his winning ticket. That's what Dominelli did. He was long and short on these transactions, and then put the winning one in his record," says Richard Rosenblatt, an investor.

"He was a loser in all those accounts, and there was knowledge of it in the community, yet those of us close to him didn't know it," laments a J. David employee who stuck with the firm until the very end and lost more than $1 million.

One reason that news of the losses didn't get very far in the community is that Dominelli and one of his lawyers made threats to some of those talking about their suspicions.

After speaking with Dominelli, Hoover, and Pulaski, San Diego foreign currency trader Ronald Brouillette didn't believe that anybody at J. David had extensive knowledge of interbank trading. "Dominelli was shaky on some details he should have known about. Hoover was paranoid about anybody with knowledge," recalls Brouillette. And he had the standard questions about the lack of confirmations and any kind of paper trail.

When asked, Brouillette would express his doubts to San Diego investors. One day, Dominelli was on the phone: "Ron, you're bad-mouthing me."

"I'm not bad-mouthing you," said Brouillette, who explained that he was recommending investors insist on the confirmations that Dominelli did not provide.

"Nancy's all shook up. If you don't stop, we're going to sue you," said Dominelli.

Next, Brouillette's lawyer called Dominelli and said, "Don't you ever call and threaten him."

It cooled off, but Dominelli had made his point.

Another San Diego interbank professional began providing his clients with audited statements, confirmations, and monthly accounting of trading positions. He used this full accounting as a sales tool, telling his potential clients that Dominelli provided no such information.

"I started getting calls from Norm Nouskajian [one of Dominelli's key lawyers]," remembers the dealer. "He said I had no right to do what I was doing. He threatened to sue. I asked him if this was Russia. Since when in America can't you compete fairly?" The dealer continued to receive threatening calls from Nouskajian, he says.

From time to time, San Diegans would get telephone inquiries about Dominelli from interbank operatives. "One major New York bank called me. They couldn't figure out why, if Dominelli did all that business in interbank, they couldn't ever find his name on the other side of the ticket," says Jack White, who runs the largest discount brokerage in San Diego. He would frequently discourage his customers from putting money in J. David's interbank fund.

People outside San Diego grew increasingly suspicious. An Oklahoma investor first contacted a J. David salesman in 1981. He was told that Dominelli's track record appeared in Yarry's *The Fastest Game in Town: Commodities*. Noting that Yarry listed himself on the book jacket as former president of the New Orleans Commodities Exchange, the investor checked it out. When told that Yarry had never been president, he held back. Several times he asked for an *audited* J. David track record and was told one would be coming soon, but it never did.

Nonetheless, in 1982, he decided to drop a little money in the pot: $50,000. But he informed J. David personnel he had several hundred thousand more that he might invest. His first monthly statement showed a handsome 4.575 percent return. The next month was a smashing 5.88, followed by 1.67. He phoned Pulaski again for the audited track record. Pulaski ducked that issue, but told the investor, "If you have that kind of money to invest, I will charter a Lear jet to La Jolla, and bring your money with you. I will show you our records and give you the names of our brokers in New York, and you can go to them and ask them about us. We have an excellent reputation with the banking firms in New York, and they all know us well. With the kind of money you have, think of how much money you are losing by not having that money with us."

"I thanked him and began for the first time to seriously question the wisdom of my investment with J. David & Company," says the investor. He turned down the free trip to La Jolla, but he continued to phone J. David personnel for more information. At the time, J. David was setting up a London operation. "One of the women there was excited about the London office. She had been there a month earlier. I asked her who would head the office. She said it would be Mark Yarry. Then I was even more convinced I would pull out my money," recalls the Oklahoman.

This investor made J. David his private investigative project. He got out the fancy J. David brochure and started calling the references. Managers of the brokerage houses for which Dominelli had worked did not seem to know him. The Oklahoman checked some interbank experts on Wall Street, and they all agreed that anybody who could make 40 to 50 percent a year over three years with only one losing month was extremely questionable.

After numerous inquiries, J. David finally sent a track record—covering the period from January 1981 to August 1982, not back to 1977, as the original track record did. "The figures given in their track record did not match the figures on my own statements," says the Oklahoman.

He passed the story to a Wall Street commodities expert, who was also incredulous. He told the expert that Drexel Burnham Lambert's name was on the monthly statements and that J. David salespeople were saying the firm was high on Dominelli. Although Drexel was a competitor, the Wall Street pro suggested the Oklahoman call John Benjamin, a Drexel commodities official in Chicago. The Oklahoman told Benjamin of J. David's unbelievable trading results and reminded him that his firm's name was on the statements and in the brochure. Benjamin was irked: He had instructed J. David not to use Drexel's name in its promotions. And he had been assured that the Drexel account was Dominelli's personal money, not customers' money. He told the Oklahoman he would check Dominelli's alleged track record against actual results at Drexel.

Meanwhile, the Oklahoman continued his calls. He specifically wanted to verify one bit of information. A J. David salesman had told him that the firm owned a "fully licensed English bank." Without identifying himself as an investor, he made calls to other J. David salesmen. Finally, one informed him that it wasn't really an English bank—it was the British subsidiary of a Montserrat bank. "It was at this time that I decided to close my account," says the Oklahoman, who did so.

But he wanted to check back with Benjamin at Drexel. As it turned out, Benjamin had found that Dominelli's highly touted track record did not jibe with his record at Drexel. "We made a minute number of trades for him, and he basically lost money," says Benjamin.

"Benjamin told me that I had made a good decision by deciding to close my account with J. David," says the Oklahoman. "He further told me that he had spoken with Mr. Dominelli personally and requested that J. David take their business elsewhere."

The Oklahoman phoned a San Diego journalist, who asked Dominelli about Drexel's action. "They did that because they are mad at us. We have hired some of their best salesmen," Dominelli explained, according to the Oklahoman.

Back in 1981 another Wall Street firm, E.F. Hutton, had turned down J. David. Frank Pusateri, then head of Hutton's foreign exchange trading, had sent one of his employees to talk with Dominelli. "He got a snow job. Lots of hype, lots of reports that were not audited, lots of unverifiable track records," recalls Pusateri.

Later Pusateri was contacted by several investors, including the Oklahoman. When he heard that Dominelli was claiming investors had made 50 percent over three years with only one losing month, Pusateri snapped, "That is a fraud." It's possible to make 50 percent over a fairly long period, but it's a rocky road. "You'll be down 50 percent part of the time," says Pusateri.

Some of Dominelli's most loyal salesmen heard from these

skeptics. A San Diego interbank sales representative who was competing with J. David took a famous Chicago foreign currency trader to see Arthur Axelrod, J. David's man in Orange County. Axelrod proudly showed the Chicago pro his monthly statements indicating steady earnings gains. The Chicago trader cocked an eyebrow at Axelrod. "How much do you want to make in a month?" he asked.

"What do you mean?" Axelrod asked back.

"I mean, do you want to make 8 percent a month? Or 12 percent a month? You name the figure and give me that typewriter over there, and I'll type it into your statement," said the trader bitingly. Axelrod had no reply.

In early 1983 Mel Shapiro, a San Diegan who suspected J. David was a scam, called John Shockey, an investigator for the Comptroller of the Currency in Washington, D.C. Shockey, one of the U.S.'s ranking experts on offshore shell banks, explained that his department had no regulatory authority over J. David Banking. Shapiro mentioned to Shockey that Dominelli had top political and social contacts, paid investors 50 percent on their money, and was becoming known as a "great local success story."

Shockey's reaction? "Fifty years ago Charles Ponzi was known as a great success story in Boston, too."

Shockey had done some investigative work on Dominelli. He found that professionals in the foreign currency market had never heard of him. Moreover, "Dominelli claimed that he did all this trading himself. No one person could possibly do all that trading alone," says Shockey. Further, Shockey believed that if J. David's interbank operation were legitimate, it wouldn't require the offshore shell bank on Montserrat.

One government official, who knew of Mark Yarry's

reputation, comments, "If you're going to run a reputable foreign exchange firm, you don't associate with someone like Mark Yarry."

Some people became suspicious by observing less recondite matters. Once Dominelli feted a group of potential investors at a very expensive San Diego restaurant. A guest took a peek at the bill: It was more than $1,000. Dominelli paid with cash, "and he never picked up the stub [for tax purposes]. Then and there I figured that something was seriously wrong," reasoned the guest, who never put a dime with J. David.

Not surprisingly, similar doubts were building inside J. David. In particular, employees wondered how Dominelli could do so well trading foreign currencies when he was so frequently not paying attention to the Telerate screen. The big banks that do the bulk of the interbank trading normally have platoons of experts watching prices twenty-four hours a day.

"But you would go into Dominelli's office, and all this excitement would be going on around the world, and prices would be moving up and down based on those momentous events, and Dominelli would be sitting there interviewing a candidate for a receptionist's job someplace in the organization," recalls a former financial official for J. David.

During trading hours, Robert Mengar would see Dominelli standing around outside his office. "I would think to myself, How can he leave? Who's doing the trading?"

In unguarded moments Dominelli told employees that results in several different months had been down—yet he had reported to customers only one losing month in three years. Based on what Dominelli had said, "I could have sworn there were more bad months," says Mengar.

There were other tip-offs. For example, Dominelli told customers that he spent up to half of their investment on conservative Treasury bills. One executive proposed that J. David set up a firm dealing in these bills: If J. David bought so many of them, it would be cheaper than buying on the market. When Dominelli killed the idea without a second's consideration, the employee—one who had openly doubted whether Dominelli was doing much trading—became even more suspicious.

Another executive noted at the time, "Jerry never takes a long vacation. That smells like an accountant who is cooking the books. The first tip-off is always that he never takes a vacation."

This employee also observed that early in J. David's existence, "Nancy got her monthly statements and Jerry's monthly statements out on the first or second of each month." The clerk who was compiling statements for other J. David traders "wouldn't get those statements out until the fifth or sixth of every month, because she was waiting for confirmations. Since we had never seen confirmations on Jerry's trades, and nobody had seen confirmations, this made us wonder even more if Jerry was actually trading."

The executive discussed the matter with the clerk. One time when Hoover was out of the office, the clerk tiptoed in and checked her "black book"—something that Dominelli insisted no one look at. "She came to me crying," the executive remembers. "She said 90 percent of the trades in Nancy's book didn't jibe with the records. She kept crying. She was a divorcée with a child. She needed the money, she said. She wasn't going to do anything." (She also had been given a new car.)

Another employee noticed something peculiar whenever a foreign currency expert would come to town and go to dinner with Dominelli and other J. David people. "When the talk about the [foreign currency] market got serious, got down to cases, that would be the time Jerry would make himself scarce. One time a noted economics professor came through and Jerry kept jumping up to make phone calls," he recalls.

The Hoover-Dominelli buying spree especially bothered several employees. Mengar did some basic arithmetic and calculated that to be spending at the level he was, Dominelli had to have well over $100 million under management—a figure Mengar found hard to believe. A financial officer of the firm came up with a similar figure, but even though he was an accountant, he was not permitted to look at the interbank fund.

Skepticism was mounting both inside and outside the company. There were whispers throughout San Diego and in the world's commodities markets.

As talk of a Ponzi scheme and money laundering escalated, one J. David functionary would gallantly—and piously—put his finger in each dike. It was George Mitrovich.

It was a case of anti-Italian bigotry, said Mitrovich, pointing out that his own roots were Yugoslavian. Did that make *him* suspect?

5

The Rape of the Regulators

Nancy Hoover's liberal colleagues believe that strong government regulation can foil the freebooters in the private sector. Jerry Dominelli's Libertarians argue that government regulation is expensive and generally ineffective.

The saga of J. David proves conclusively that both are right—and wrong.

The fact that J. David succeeded as long as it did is a powerful argument for strong government regulation of the marketplace. The fact that J. David completely eluded federal and state regulators is an equally powerful argument that government regulation is a waste of time and money.

Picture Luciano Pavarotti whipping the competition in the 220-yard hurdles at the Olympics. Or Boy George stiff-arming and bowling over the defense of the Los Angeles Raiders. Now you have an idea of what J. David did to federal and state regulatory agencies: It ran past them and over them. To accomplish the heroics, Dominelli had expert downfield blocking from his lawyers and accountants.

Dubious moves abounded, but nobody dropped a handkerchief until it was too late—at least for many investors.

J. David's first brush with the regulators came in 1981 after a money-finder sent a sales brochure into the state of Missouri. Authorities in that state questioned whether the offerings were registered as securities. (Under the law, a "security" is basically an investment contract in which the profits result from the management expertise of people other than the investor.)

Missouri took action against J. David, which hired Abramson & Fox, a prestigious Chicago law firm, as counsel. Soon Missouri tipped off California, and the California Department of Corporations was questioning Carl Duncan, an Abramson & Fox attorney (and former SEC official) about the J. David sales contract. Beginning in mid-1981, Duncan and George Crawford, corporations counsel of the California Department of Corporations, exchanged long letters outlining their positions on the question.

In July 1981 Dominelli promised he would sell no more commodity programs until the matter was resolved. While the barrister and the bureaucrat were engaged in their bombastic correspondence, Dominelli was just shifting gears: With Hoover and Yarry, he was plotting a new sales strategy—and he wasn't telling Duncan about it.

Crawford and Duncan agreed that J. David's selling of conventional commodity partnerships was not in compliance with applicable state and federal securities laws, and more than a year later, in late 1982, J. David was forced to make an expensive rescission agreement. In effect, Dominelli had to give his investors their money back, if they wanted it.

This was the same period that Dominelli ran afoul of the

Commodity Futures Trading Commission (CFTC). After a mid-1982 examination, the CFTC questioned whether Dominelli was correctly segregating clients' funds from corporate funds. It noted that J. David failed to file annual reports of certain trading pools and did not keep adequate daily records of commodity interest transactions. The CFTC also pointed to a number of accounting deficiencies.

Duncan admitted most of the irregularities, and in a letter of September 29, 1982, pleaded with the CFTC supervisor, "Since its [inception], J. David & Company has sought to comply with both the spirit and the specifics of applicable CFTC regulations. While the spirit has been met, in all candor the detail has not been met in every instance. Much of the deficiencies outlined herein arose because of insufficient operational follow-up and confusion as to the specificity expected by the CFTC during the period. . . . Significant efforts recently have been taken to remedy such difficulties." Duncan asked that no staff action be taken against J. David, stressing that "no irreparable public harm has resulted" from J. David's inadequate accounting procedures. He promised that Dominelli would "remedy the deficiencies," and, after all, he pointed out, Dominelli had not been selling his commodity programs since July 1981.

Duncan apparently believed all that. But Dominelli was plunging ahead.

The seed? A lawyer's casual remark to Dominelli that if he truly wanted to be free of regulation, he should operate exclusively in interbank foreign currency trading. The result? Dominelli was preparing to enter that business, no matter what Duncan was telling governmental bodies.

The foreign currency market is an ancient market. As long as human beings have been doing business across national borders, there has been trading in national currencies. Until this century, the external values of currencies were normally expressed in gold or silver. But there were problems: When a country had to finance a war, it had to find more gold or it would run out of money and therefore out of weapons. And so in wartime, countries temporarily went off the gold standard and had nothing backing up their currencies. This held the potential for chaos.

In 1944, in an attempt to stabilize the situation, the world adopted the Bretton Woods system. All currencies would henceforth be valued in terms of the U.S. dollar, which would be valued in terms of gold. Other currencies would trade in very narrow, fixed ranges relative to one another. One important feature of the system: Any time a country collected thirty-five U.S. dollars, it could turn them back to the U.S. for one ounce of gold.

For years after World War II, there was a shortage of U.S. dollars abroad, known as "the dollar gap." But then the U.S. kept sending more and more U.S. dollars overseas, as its companies bought up foreign assets, its people traveled heavily in nations with cheap currencies, and it financed overseas military operations, as in Vietnam. The gap became a glut. Foreign countries were gobbling up American gold—in fact, overseas governments had more dollars than the U.S. had gold. Foreign central banks, brokers, commercial banks, individuals, and corporations all held piles of dollars. They looked for places to earn interest on those dollars, but the U.S. had artificially low interest rates: The Federal Reserve limited the rate offered by savings institutions. And it was illegal to pay interest on checking accounts.

As a result, the phenomenon known as the "Eurodollar market" mushroomed. A Eurodollar is nothing more than a dollar on deposit in a bank outside the U.S. The Eurodollar market started as a kind of dollar market in exile. With all those dollars looking for an interest-paying home, American banks saw a chance to expand the market. They set up shell banks or subsidiaries with skeleton staffs in Caribbean tax havens. These "banks" were primarily accounting vehicles to permit the big banks to create Eurodollars without regulation by the U.S., without having to meet U.S. reserve requirements (keeping some dollars on hand to back up those lent out) or pay equivalent U.S. taxes. Most importantly, Eurodollar deposits could earn the interest that by law could not be paid by domestic banks.

By the early 1970s, the dollar glut became an acute danger to the U.S. economy. On August 15, 1971, President Nixon declared that the U.S. would no longer sell gold to foreign governments in exchange for dollars. With the gold backing gone, all currencies were free to "float": to trade against another currency at whatever price a person was willing to pay.

It was a marvelous opportunity for speculators. Why fool with stocks and bonds and puts and calls and wheat and pork bellies and gold and platinum when you could just speculate in, say, the French franc against the Swiss franc or the Canadian dollar against the U.S. dollar? The currency trading market exploded.

As huge as it has become, interbank trading filters into a pretty small bottle. At its center are the world's largest private banks, such as Chase Manhattan, Citibank, and Bank of America. The banks place orders for large and small corporations, governments, and other institutions that have to swap currencies. For example, the Milwaukee brewery selling its beer in France doesn't want to be paid in the French franc. (It's hard to pay for a sandwich with a French franc in Milwaukee.) So the French importer agrees to pay the Milwaukee brewery in U.S. dollars, and a bank turns his francs into dollars. There are dealers (such as brokerage firms) that do business through the big money-center banks, but essentially the world's biggest banks do the trading.

Banks and interbank pros would like us to believe that most foreign exchange trades are strictly for business purposes. But that's nonsense. High rollers all over the world—individuals, institutions, and the banks themselves—speculate on currencies. (Two big banks, New York's Franklin National and West Germany's Bankhaus I.D. Herstatt, collapsed in 1974 as a result of injudicious foreign currency gambling. The banks are doing less speculating now, but institutions and individuals are doing more.)

Foreign currency speculation is titillating because there are so many variables involved. It's the difference between a trifecta and a one-horse bet at the track. A country's currency goes up or down based on its balance of payments, current inflation and the market's expectation of future inflation, money supply data, government fiscal policy, political stability, and a host of other factors. And all these variables in *one* country have to be weighed against a similar set of variables in *another* country.

In earlier days foreign currency traders were not considered mental heavyweights. "We used to consider them even dumber than stock-and-bond traders," says one international banker. But in recent years, as the foreign currency market has boomed, highly trained economists, backed up by rows and rows of computers, have moved into the field. The expert in foreign currency needs a great deal of knowledge, and that's why so many of the foreign currency experts today, even traders, are scholars, graduates of Harvard or Cambridge, fellows with thick glasses, vested suits, and idiosyncrasies that are tolerated because these guys are, after all, geniuses.

"Jerry fit right in with the image of the interbank trader," says one of his former salesmen.

And interbank fit right in with Jerry. It was unregulated—just what he wanted.

In spring 1981 Dominelli heard, possibly from Yarry, about Jerome Schneider, a Los Angeles entrepreneur in his thirties who sells offshore shell banks. Intrigued, Captain Money and the Golden Girl—perhaps the most impulsive impulse buyers in the West—decided they just *had* to have one. They shelled out $40,000 for their own Caribbean bank, on the island of Montserrat. At first it was mainly ornamental—an in-house ego massager. "Nancy was just thrilled to own a bank," recalls a former executive. Hoover's daughter is said to have written a school paper identifying her mother as the world's first female international banker.

A few months later, someone—probably Yarry—suggested that J. David start using its "bank." So Dominelli and Hoover paid $870 to send two employees to a seminar at which Schneider expatiated on the wonders of having one's own offshore shell bank. Schneider defines his merchandise in this way: "An offshore bank is a corporation organized and licensed under the banking laws of a foreign jurisdiction which is conducive to conducting international financial transactions with minimal tax, banking, and security regulations."

There are more than one hundred promoters around the world who sell shell banks in such tax havens as Anguilla, Montserrat, Antigua, the Cayman Islands, and Saipan. The promoters get the license through the tax haven's legislature and arrange to have a local lawyer hang the plaque in his office. In selling the bank, they explain that, after all, everybody does it: If Chase Manhattan can avoid taxes and regulation by setting up subsidiaries all over the Caribbean, and Merrill Lynch can have operations in Panama, why can't you do the same for the same reasons?

Schneider, for one, contends that his company, WFI Corp., is aboveboard and that he even checks out clients for criminal backgrounds. But Schneider himself has a criminal background: In 1972 he pleaded guilty to stealing more than $200,000 in telephone equipment. He spent sixty days in jail. Los Angeles officials later sued Schneider for failing to substantiate claims he made in *Wall Street Journal* ads. He paid $2,500 and agreed to stop the misleading advertising.

Dominelli completed the paperwork for the bank in September 1981. He owned 225,000 shares, Hoover 45,000, and Yarry, who became managing director, 30,000. It was christened J. David Banking, and Parin Columna, the handyman and factotum who would loom large in later adventures, put up beautiful glass partitions etched with the bank's name outside Yarry's office.

J. David Banking was to be the means through which J. David's customers reportedly traded in interbank. The U.S. government would be told that all of the firm's foreign currency transactions were taking place via Montserrat.

Eventually Dominelli, Hoover, and Yarry planned to do all their secret, unaudited investing in the unregulated foreign currency market. This covert activity would be the source of the hush-hush funds coming from "the magic checkbook" and "Dominelli Airlines." The existing regulated commodity pools would be folded into interbank or closed out. The only J. David activities that would be regulated would be the diversified operations such as J. David Securities.

In the transition, Dominelli used the Montserrat bank for some accounting hocus-pocus with the existing commodity partnerships. In 1982 the accounting firm of Laventhol & Horwath was working on the books of a J. David commodity pool; the accountant wrote in his notes, "Due to a Montserrat statute relevant to bank confidentiality, the records of J. David Banking could not be examined."

Because of the Montserrat law—and just as Dominelli wanted—J. David Banking had no auditor. On the last day of 1981, according to the internal document, all of the partnership's funds were transferred to the bank and thus could not be audited.

Not to worry. Laventhol & Horwath could hire Norman Nouskajian, one of J. David's lawyers. *He* would peek at the books of the Montserrat bank, thus skirting Montserrat's prohibition. Nouskajian took the peek and reported his findings to Laventhol & Horwath. The accounting firm, in pronouncing everything in order, did not tell the CFTC that it had taken this dubious detour—called a "scope limitation" in accounting parlance—in its pursuit of truth. It gave the commodity pool a "clean" opinion on the basis of information supplied by J. David's own lawyer.

To make it all official, Dominelli wrote a letter to Laventhol & Horwath and stated formally, "Under a Montserrat statute relevant to bank confidentiality, transactions
between the Partnership and J. David Banking Company
Limited (Banking) and the income reported by Banking
were not examined by you. We understand that alternative procedures were used to independently substantiate the
aforementioned transactions. In this connection, it is our
opinion that the amounts recorded by the Partnership are
correct and represent all of the transactions for the period
entered into by Banking on behalf of the Partnership."

While this was going on with the existing pools, Dominelli's salesmen were aggressively bringing in money for
the interbank pool, which was paying its investors returns
of 4 percent a month. Soon the San Diego newspapers and
the *Los Angeles Times* started taking a look at J. David.
The reclusive Dominelli said almost nothing, but Hoover
gabbed with the reporters and Yarry talked openly about
the company's rapid ascent. By late 1982 all the major dai-
lies had done J. David stories.

Consequently, the California Department of Corporations got interested again. George Crawford wrote Carl
Duncan anew and demanded to know if Dominelli was
selling securities, as he promised he wouldn't. At this point,
Duncan was letting his unhappiness be known. So Dominelli turned the matter over to Rogers & Wells, one of the
nation's larger law firms, which was then working on other
matters for J. David. Rogers & Wells handles Wall Street's
giant Merrill Lynch and is famous for its securities expertise. The prestigious firm is headed by William P. Rogers,
former Secretary of State, who worked on the J. David account.

The firm's lawyers studied Dominelli's situation thoroughly. They evidently concluded that J. David was selling securities illegally in California. On January 21, 1983, a group of Rogers & Wells lawyers met with Dominelli, Yarry, Hoover, and Fred Storm, an in-house attorney.

According to notes taken at the meeting, Don Augustine, an attorney at the local office of Rogers & Wells, asked Dominelli, "Why did you embark on your course of action in accepting [client] 'pooled' accounts in California in apparent violation of law?" The lawyers explained that there would be little problem if the securities had been sold only to foreigners. (The fact was, though, they were being sold to U.S. citizens and residents.) Dominelli was told he had to (as the notes put it) "decide to/or not to" sell to Americans.

One lawyer asked, "What do we tell Mr. Crawford at DOC [the California Department of Corporations]? How do we handle containment of the issue?" They discussed precedents related to Bernard Cornfeld, whose notorious Fund of Funds had been the largest financial scandal of the early 1970s. The amanuensis recorded the consensus of the lawyers: "Don't reply in *writing*. Go up to L.A. & talk about the [Department of Corporations] investigation."

Yarry is recorded as having commented at the meeting, "What if we stop raising any new $, *none,* from Jan. 22, 1983. Still have problems!"

Then, Rogers & Wells made it official in a hand-delivered letter to Dominelli. Augustine reiterated that Rogers & Wells believed the accounts sold by Dominelli were securities which had to be registered or specifically exempted. Moreover, the accounts could only be sold in California by "individuals licensed to sell securities in the

State of California"—and Mark Yarry was not so licensed. Augustine reminded Dominelli that "until such time as appropriate legal procedures are established" for selling the interbank contracts in the U.S., Dominelli could sell interbank only outside of California "and from states where no licensing is required to market the accounts to non-resident aliens."

Finally, Augustine assured Dominelli, "While there may be past violations of the California securities laws which may also create civil liability, we have no intention of discussing these matters with Mr. Crawford."

Augustine went up to Los Angeles to talk with Crawford. In an internal memorandum, Augustine later related how he told Crawford that J. David operated with "individual discretionary accounts"—accounts in which both U.S. and foreign investors could call their own shots, with only advisory help from Dominelli through the Montserrat "bank." According to the memorandum, Crawford then opined that Dominelli's interbank contracts "were not a security but rather, as far as California was concerned, a commodity and it was the Commodity Futures Trading Commission, under the Commodities Exchange Act, which had exclusive jurisdiction."

The Rogers & Wells lawyers donned blinders. Augustine wrote an internal memorandum to Nouskajian and noted, "I do not believe it is appropriate for any member of our law firm in their capacities as attorneys to become aware of the names of the individuals who have accounts with [J. David Banking]." See no evil, hear no evil.

Under penalty of perjury, Dominelli signed a remarkable document shot full of dubious assertions. For example, Dominelli asseverated, "At this time [J. David Banking] is not accepting any accounts from other than non-resident aliens of the United States." But even after Rogers & Wells told him in January that selling interbank to Americans was illegal, Dominelli had never stopped the marketing practice. In the document, Dominelli also contended that his customers got access to the sanctum of interbank traders through the Montserrat brass-plate "bank"—an absurd statement. Dominelli said that he only made trading "recommendations" to the officers of his Montserrat "bank," who would then decide whether Dominelli's customers would follow the advice. Such a set-up would have been a cumbersome arrangement indeed for the split-second buying and selling that characterize interbank! Actually, Dominelli had told his customers that *he* did the trading for them—that *he* had the trading discretion. The document also maintained that Dominelli's bank had an "independent" board of directors. That, too, was nonsense. Yarry headed the bank, and the "independent" board members were cronies of the Montserrat lawyer in whose office the brass plate hung.

Augustine then forwarded Dominelli's sworn statement to Crawford. In an official letter, Crawford wrote, "In view of Mr. Dominelli's undertaking, twice-repeated, to comply with the state's securities laws, we anticipate no further action will be necessary to enforce the state's securities laws." So the interbank contracts, though clearly securities, were suddenly declared to be commodities, and they went unregistered. J. David continued selling them to Americans, and Rogers & Wells continued representing J. David. After the collapse, the CFTC claimed that it had never had jurisdiction over the matter.

"The state of California was very foolish," complains a

J. David lawyer who advised Dominelli that he was in fact dealing in securities that had to be registered.

George Crawford would later stonewall. Asked why the Department of Corporations had not ruled that Dominelli was selling securities, Crawford replied, "We will have no comment to avoid prejudicing the effect of further litigation." His unusual argument was that the Department of Corporations is empowered to be cocounsel in prosecution of certain offenders, and that if he discussed why his department didn't move in on Dominelli, it would harm the department's possible role in future prosecution.

With the Department of Corporations taken care of, J. David brass had cause to celebrate. But the cork was barely out of the champagne bottle when employees were tipped off to more trouble. Parin Columna took down the glass panel outside Yarry's office with the J. David Banking sign on it. Sure enough, another agency had raised its head: the California Banking Department. What was this J. David Banking? Was it doing business in California? If it was doing any business at all in the state—not just banking business—it had to register, said the Banking Department. But Yarry assured an examiner from the Banking Department that no deposits were taken in La Jolla. And Dominelli, through Rogers & Wells, told the state that the company did no business in California—that all its customers were foreigners and no business whatsoever was conducted within the state, that everything happened on Montserrat and in J. David's London office. Again, this was complete nonsense. The American investors in J. David made out checks to J. David Banking and normally turned them over to J. David at its La Jolla headquarters. Investors were told the checks were sent to Great Britain and endorsed there.

One San Diego law firm, pressing a claim against a minor J. David functionary, apprised the Banking Department investigator that J. David collected funds in La Jolla. The Banking Department also knew of a lawsuit filed against J. David by a former money-finder who had plied his trade within California. But J. David's lead bank, San Diego's First National, dutifully wrote the Banking Department that all checks written to J. David Banking in the previous month had been endorsed by signatories overseas and that the statements were sent to Montserrat.

For still-unexplained reasons the Banking Department retreated. "We made an investigation of J. David Banking in 1983 and we were unable to determine that [it] was doing business in the state," says Alida Buchanan, the Banking Department counsel. Had the department known that J. David routinely accepted deposits in La Jolla, it would have ruled differently, she allows, "but we didn't have that information."

Some observers are very critical of the state regulators, and rightly so. "The lies [by Dominelli] to the state regulators were transparent," says a prominent San Diego attorney. "Virtually any on-site investigation, check of customer lists, or the like would have exposed the whole thing. Interviews with ex-employees, or even honest current employees, would have done the same. At the state level, I wonder if political influence—or worse—might have been involved. But I have absolutely no evidence."

The federal government stumbled, too. The Treasury Department was suspicious but believed it had no authority. Evidence suggests the SEC conducted a formal probe of J. David's interbank in the 1982–1983 period, but closed it. (Later, the agency admitted having destroyed its J. David file.) It definitely launched an investigation *after* the collapse. The IRS, of course, was regularly checking into J. David, but if it found anything amiss, it never made it public until more than a year after J. David's downfall.

The FBI got in early. When John Shockey, investigator for the Comptroller of the Currency, became suspicious of J. David in early 1983, he passed on information to the San Diego branch of the FBI, which had already received complaints from ex-employees of the firm. An investigator interviewed a number of people connected with J. David. Several told the agent it was a Ponzi scheme. One agent said to an ex-employee, "It looks like a Ponzi scheme and smells like a Ponzi scheme." But, he continued, "I don't want to be responsible for tearing down a viable business."

Dominelli was aware of the FBI investigation and, at one point in the fall of 1983, emerged from his office to assure employees, "They're just looking for drug money."

According to an ex-employee, in early 1984 J. David attorney Mike Clark took FBI investigator Roger Dodd through the posh J. David office. "Dodd said they were the most beautiful offices he had ever seen," the former employee remembers. On January 15, he says, the FBI closed the case—only to reopen it a few weeks later when the company collapsed.

The FBI tells a different story. It couldn't believe the 40–50 percent annual returns and the three straight winning years with only one losing month, and it had received complaints from two former employees, "but we didn't have a victim," says an FBI official. That, he contends, prevented the FBI from taking certain legal steps. It never officially closed the case, "but came close," he admits, in early 1984. As for Dominelli's "drug money" statement, he says that the FBI was not looking for drug money prior to the firm's collapse, but that it later investigated possible drug-money laundering.

One high-level federal official believes there is more to why the FBI didn't move fast: Dominelli and Hoover had so many powerful political friends that the FBI, which is often sensitive to political criticism, was too cautious in pursuing the case.

Other public and private institutions were told about what was happening at J. David, but did nothing. The experience of the Oklahoma investor who had pulled out his money is eloquent. He called the San Diego reporters who were in the midst of their preliminary investigations of J. David in 1982. Alas, little of what he told them got into print. He called the Commodity Futures Trading Commission and the SEC, and was informed by both that interbank trading was unregulated. He called the National Futures Association, a private watchdog group then being formed, which let him know that the only action it could take would be to terminate J. David's membership in the group. He called the U.S. Senate Permanent Subcommittee on Investigations and spilled his story. He was given a polite hearing and nothing more. He called a producer of TV's "60 Minutes," but couldn't interest anyone. Sighed the Oklahoman at the time, "This guy is pulling a scam. Doesn't anybody give a damn?"

The federal government *did* give a damn, it turns out. On July 21, 1980, the United States of America moved decisively against J. David "Jerry" Dominelli. It sued him for $2,313.41 for having defaulted on two student loans in 1968 and 1969. But except for that $2,000 and change, the federal government felt it had no authority.

Occasionally word leaked out of the J. David inner circle that there were regulatory strains. For example, Edith Reid, the head of Reid-Smith (the firm pooling small investors' funds to reach Dominelli's $50,000 minimum), picked up whispers in late 1983 that J. David was not cooperating with regulatory agencies. She got a polite note from Gary H. Wiles of Wiles, Circuit & Tremblay, a law firm representing J. David. "You expressed your concerns to Michael Clark of this firm concerning the purported failure of J. David Co. to cooperate with regulatory agencies," wrote Wiles. He then ticked off recent satisfactory tests. The National Association of Securities Dealers (NASD), which regulates over-the-counter securities firms, had conducted an audit "and found only minor technical difficulties." The National Futures Association (NFA) had also noted, according to Wiles, only "minor technical difficulties." (The NFA would later claim, however, that it wasn't permitted to look into J. David.) The SEC and CFTC were also performing routine annual audits, and J. David was not concerned. "Based on the foregoing, it appears that this company is in a business that is perhaps more highly regulated than any other usual business pursuit and there is no evidence whatsoever to date of any failure of the company to comply with audit requirements or to furnish information to the auditing or investigating agencies," said Wiles.

Wiles was missing the point. It was true that the SEC, CFTC, NASD, and other public and private regulatory groups *had* looked at J. David. But, in the main, they had officially looked at only those parts of the organization that were operating in *regulated* markets, such as J. David Securities and J. David Mercantile. But this was just a small portion of J. David. The big apple—rotten to its core—was the interbank foreign-currency trading fund. *It* was audited by no one—not a government agency, not a private regulatory body, nor even anyone inside J. David. As San Diego lawyer Michael Aguirre succinctly observes, "Dominelli represented self-deregulation."

6

The Clients Get Fleeced.
The U.K. Gets Wise

Despite widespread cynicism about Dominelli both inside and outside San Diego—and inside and outside the government—J. David had many avid supporters. Dominelli and Hoover each had a natural constituency (his conservative, hers liberal), and the sales force and money-finders had *their* own constituencies (mainly ordinary people who wanted to make a bundle of money without paying taxes on it). And J. David had friends in high places—top-level politicians and reputable service professionals who gave it credibility.

Foremost among the politicians was Roger Hedgecock. Financed heavily by Hoover and Dominelli, he had been elected mayor of San Diego in 1983. On his first day in office, in May of that year, he called Captain Money and the Golden Girl at their La Jolla office. "I'm really here. I'm sitting at the mayor's desk. I'm in the mayor's private office. I'm on the mayor's private phone. And it's great. I'm having a ball." Later in the day, Dominelli threw a magnificent inaugural party at the Hilton for one thousand guests. Floating in the swimming pool was an ice sculpture proclaiming "San Diego Loves Roger Hedgecock."

Hedgecock was a J. David investor, and so were numerous other Beautiful People from the world of politics. James Mills, former president pro tem of the California State Senate, chipped in. So did Simon Casady, social activist and former liberal candidate for mayor of San Diego. And Deborah Szekely, a wealthy and socially prominent spa owner who had tried to get the Republican nomination for a seat in Congress.

The son of M. Larry Lawrence, former chairman of the California Democratic Party, jumped aboard. So did Carl Ludlow, a former campaign manager for Hedgecock. And Murray L. Galinson, an aide to Walter Mondale. And Lowell Blankfort, a liberal journalist who had made millions publishing a small San Diego suburban daily.

There were two judges: San Diego Superior Court Judge Michael Greer; and El Cajon Municipal Court Judge Victor Bianchini, an ex-Marine who got in through Pulaski. And—though he hardly added to J. David's respectability—former Michigan judge James Del Rio, who had moved to California after being defrocked by the Michigan Judicial Tenure Commission on charges of judicial misconduct. (Among other offenses, he had boasted from the bench of his sexual prowess.)

James Mills said his $50,000 investment represented 20 percent of his net worth. "I got into it because quite a number of people I knew and trusted, who knew Dominelli personally and had high opinions of him, basically vouched for the safety. Besides, I've known Nancy Hoover for years and felt that whatever she was involved in was on the strait and narrow."

Simon Casady got in with $40,000—less than the $50,000 minimum—because of his friendship with people inside the organization, he says. "I've known Nancy Hoover for a long time. Her daughter and my granddaughter are friends. Over the vociferous protests of my wife and children, I sneaked down to J. David and paid my money."

Even more important than the political support were J. David's professional associations. It had Rogers & Wells, the nation's thirty-second largest law firm, and Wiles, Circuit & Tremblay, a smaller local firm. It had Laventhol & Horwath, the nation's eleventh largest accounting firm. Its lead bank was First National of San Diego, a relatively young but well-capitalized and ultra-establishment-backed institution. First National handled J. David's checking, gave it a mortgage on its headquarters, offered it a big loan at the prime rate, and loaned money to Yarry and other individuals.

These high-powered relationships were important. "It couldn't be a Ponzi scheme. Rogers & Wells was there," Mills says. "This was a major consideration in a lot of people's thinking."

"Laventhol & Horwath. Rogers & Wells. That was enough for me," says investor Leon Becker, a memorabilia dealer who did business with Dominelli.

And J. David could boast that it worked through major U.S. brokerages. Trades for J. David Securities were cleared through Wall Street's Bear, Stearns, which enjoys a good reputation. Commodities trades in regulated markets were cleared through Refco and through Goodman, Manaster— Chicago firms with credibility.

Relationships of the interbank fund with brokerage houses were extremely fragile: The J. David account had been jettisoned by Bache, Drexel, and Merrill Lynch. Nonetheless, J. David salespeople and brochures bragged about the firm's positive relationship with these national brokerages.

Sales personnel also made much of the $10 million bond from Chubb Corporation protecting investors against internal fraud. They would refer prospective investors to Ron Massa, a San Francisco–based agent of Rollins Burdick & Hunter, the large insurance agency. He had sold the bond to Dominelli. He also had a position in Dominelli's foreign exchange fund, and some people believe he got a break in his stake—that he was permitted to put in less than the $50,000 minimum or received some other concession. Massa acknowledges he had a position in interbank, but refuses to say whether he was given favorable terms.

Interbank salespeople would claim that individual investors could also obtain a personal policy guaranteeing their account. But they were touting such coverage long after the insurer had abolished it. And Chubb had no intention of renewing the corporate bond on J. David, because Dominelli would not reveal the total amount of investor funds on deposit or where they were located. The salespeople, though, were prepared for the coming policy cancellation. They told potential investors that J. David was also backed by Lloyd's of London. It wasn't.

Dominelli's hatred of tax collectors endeared him to the antitax crowd. Much evidence indicates that Dominelli was running his own subterranean economy, paying for products and services by giving the vendor a position in interbank rather than writing out a check. It has not been determined whether the recipients paid taxes on the income.

In an examination by the bankruptcy trustee, Dominelli later admitted that he reimbursed Norman Nouskajian by giving him a $12,000 position in the interbank fund in return for "just personal services, really, personal service, you know, separate from, you know, legal fees earned by his firm." He also explained that he had told Robert Harlan, another of his attorneys, to sell a 1980 Rolls-Royce, a 500 SEL Mercedes, and "a couple of Ferraris" that Dominelli owned to cover legal fees and other expenses.

Jay Gordon was given a $600,000 position in interbank in exchange for selling his company, Teachersworth Services, to J. David. "For every fifty or a hundred thousand dollars in commissions that he would produce, he would get—he'd be able to withdraw that amount from that account," Dominelli explained to lawyers for the bankruptcy trustee.

Dominelli was a lover of historical documents, letters of famous people, and other collectibles. Memorabilia dealer Becker, who provided Dominelli with such items, also had a substantial position in interbank. When interviewed by the bankruptcy trustee, Dominelli insisted that Becker was not reimbursed through an interbank account. But Becker unhesitatingly acknowledges that Dominelli paid for the merchandise by giving him an interbank position, although, Becker says, he recorded such sales as income and paid taxes on them.

Athletes and entertainers were also big investors in interbank. Mark Allen and Scott Tinley, two Team J. David triathletes, were in the pot. So was Frank Shorter, the famed

Olympic long-distance runner. He was impressed with the company's sponsorship of Team J. David, and put $163,000 in through salesman and triathlete champ Ted Pulaski. "It's sad that a lot of us got taken. But the people who have really been made to suffer were some of those young triathletes who invested everything they had when they couldn't afford to. It makes it so much sadder," says Shorter.

Comedian Joey Bishop got in, as did Dr. Michael Resnick, a San Diego physician and local TV commentator on health topics. Singer Enzo Stuarti, who was building a $1 million home in Palm Springs, got in through Transatlantic's Arthur Axelrod. "My life and career have been affected emotionally by this," comments Stuarti. "You know they tell you, 'Trust thy fellow man,' but after something like this, you say, 'How far should I trust anybody?' "

Thomas DiNoto, a TV jingle writer, is head of a firm that in 1982 won a multimillion-dollar antitrust judgment. A lifelong friend of Norman Nouskajian, DiNoto in late 1983 put $2 million of his money into J. David, hoping to build up a diversified portfolio in bonds, commodities, and speculative currency trading. More than half of it ($1.2 million) wound up in the interbank foreign currency account. Despite his friendship with Nouskajian—now exceedingly strained—DiNoto was the first to sue Dominelli when J. David began to crash.

An investor known in entertainment—and law enforcement—circles was Allen R. Glick of La Jolla, a former owner of four Las Vegas casinos that figured in a federal investigation of money skimming by mobsters. (Glick was never indicted.) Glick, who knew Dominelli and other J. David associates socially, had more than $500,000 in interbank and pulled it out after amassing a nice profit. Glick also put more than $100,000 in Yuba Natural Resources through Dominelli.

Well known among the local elite are Orange County investors James Beauchamp, Dr. Robert Beauchamp, and Bob Ganiere. Dr. Robert Beauchamp's company, Dental Finance, along with James Beauchamp and Ganiere, owned an Orange County insurance firm, Independent Indemnity, which had more than 40 percent of its $4 million in assets invested in the J. David interbank fund. Indeed, the insurance company dropped $1.1 million into the fund only a few days before J. David collapsed. The California Department of Insurance, justifiably horrified by the imprudence of such an investment, later declared the company "hopelessly insolvent" and took it over, rescuing the policyholders.

Independent Indemnity wasn't the sole example of astoundingly imprudent investing. Although pensions are supposed to be extremely conservative investments, more than a dozen pension funds of various descriptions got into the interbank fund. Most were pension programs for doctors, lawyers, and their employees, but some were for corporations. One corporation was Chicago's Victor Business Forms, the Dominelli family business. There was also the retirement fund of Richard Dominelli, one of Jerry's brothers.

Another company that bet its pension fund on Captain Money was INESCO (International Nuclear Energy Systems) of La Jolla, which was trying to develop a small nuclear fusion reactor. J. David money-finder Asher Schapiro and J. David investor Richard Rosenblatt were both on its board. INESCO put $250,000 of pension-fund money in interbank, and the two top officers sunk $350,000 be-

Nancy Hoover towered over Jerry Dominelli in almost every respect: physique, status, personal charm and wit, community influence and acceptance. This photo was taken at the La Jolla office of J. David & Company in November 1982, at the beginning of the big surge that brought in most of the $200 million the firm received from investors.

Some of the money "invested" in J. David was spent to indulge Hoover's fondness for furs and fast foreign cars.

The Dominelli-Hoover estate in affluent Rancho Santa Fe, just north of San Diego, was worth more than $2 million.

Dominelli and Hoover used investors' money to live out fantasies of public philanthropy as well as personal luxury. They contributed $187,500 to the multimillion-dollar Mandell Weiss Center for the Performing Arts at the University of California–San Diego and also gave liberally to the San Diego Symphony, the San Diego Opera, and various charities.

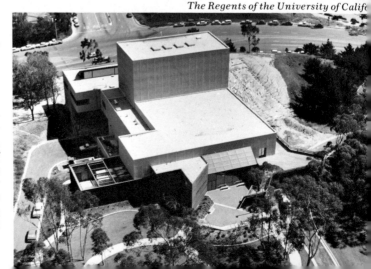

This La Jolla building, owned by J. David, housed the well-appointed offices of Dominelli and Hoover, as well as those of Mark Yarry and George Mitrovich. Yarry (*below left*), head of J. David Banking, was part of the triumvirate that ran J. David & Company. Mitrovich (*below right*) was J. David's public- and community-relations director.

Even as the J. David fantasy unraveled, Dominelli and Hoover partied. They are seen here at a Rancho Santa Fe party in mid-December 1983, after the run on J. David had already started.

The run on J. David turned into an avalanche soon after a newspaper story accompanied by this photo of Dominelli's empty office was published on January 27, 1984.

hotos this page—Dennis Huls, Union-Tribune Publishing Co.

Not long after investors sued to place J. David in bankruptcy in February 1984, it was revealed that San Diego mayor Roger Hedgecock was an investor, with various ties to the company and to Hoover. At a press conference (*above*), Hedgecock displays records of part of his J. David involvement.

Before a court hearing in San Diego on March 4, 1984, Dominelli is alone with his thoughts.

Just before the company went into bankruptcy, Dominelli, Hoover, and several of their lieutenants stuffed corporate records—what there were of them—into trash bags and stashed them in garages in San Diego and Orange counties. After the bankruptcy, some of the records were turned over to the court in downtown San Diego, as seen in this photo of March 16, 1984.

Dominelli fled to the West Indies island of Montserrat in April 1984, claiming he would pay back investors from there. Instead, things got worse, and on April 27, television viewers in San Diego—and nationwide—saw Dominelli arrested for illegal possession of firearms (*above*). Eventually Montserrat authorities expelled Dominelli, and he was returned to San Diego on May 1, 1984 (*below*).

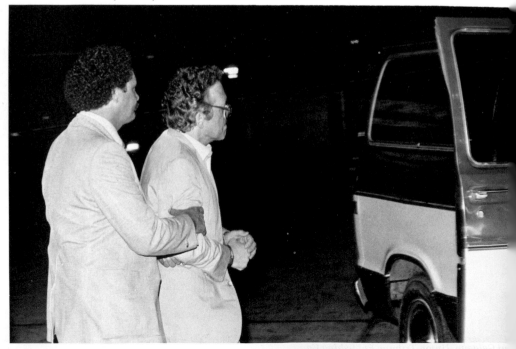

ABOVE: In November 1984 the bankruptcy trustee raised funds by auctioning off some of Dominelli's and Hoover's assets—sports cars, furs, jewelry, collectibles. BELOW: In dark glasses and somber mood, Hoover attended the auction with her son, Georgie (*to her right*).

long in Dec
e family and
art of the
esponsible

e other side
much I

thoughts abou
cers, I sup-
re for the

the same
could come
not be a
better person, or at least a more sensitive one.
Nance, thanks for all the loving moments, without them, I'd have been nothin
more than another Darth Vader.
And although you may not believe
it, and rightfully so, I love you beyond
what can be expressed in words.

Jerry

Before his departure for Montserrat in April 1984, Dominelli had written a tender three-page letter to Hoover. After his incarceration at the San Diego Metropolitan Correction Center, he made collect calls—mostly to Hoover—every 20 to 30 minutes during daylight hours. In the course of one such call to Hoover, on October 2, 1984, Dominelli suffered a debilitating stroke.

tween them into the pot. In addition, a group of employees had $300,000 in the fund, administered gratis by INESCO. The company collapsed not long after J. David's demise, for largely unrelated reasons.

Then there was the Decatur, Illinois–based Preachers Aid Society, which handles pensions for eight hundred retired Methodist ministers. Founded in 1869, the Society has a "balanced portfolio" of investments in farmland, stocks and bonds, and mortgages, but keeps a modest amount of money on the side to take an occasional run at a highflier, explains Dr. Vernie T. Barnett, executive secretary. "We checked out the Dominelli bank thoroughly before depositing any money there," he asserts. Eventually, the Preachers Aid Society plunked down $681,759.42. Barnett and his wife liked interbank so much that they put some of their own money into a side deal.

And there was the Universal Life Church. It put $15,000 into interbank for its pastor pension fund. However, the Universal Life Church has a rather spotty record. A strict semanticist might put quotation marks around "church," in rather the way Dominelli's Montserrat-based fantasy is correctly identified as a "bank." The Universal Life Church is a mail-order operation: It sends out minister's credentials for two dollars; for five dollars a member can attain sainthood. The government has been bedeviled by the organization for years, claiming that people join to avoid the draft or taxes, or both, or for various other purposes. The branch of the Universal Life Church that invested with Dominelli remains a mystery, because there is no church of any kind located at the address listed on the investor's check.

The clergy weren't the only professionals to get into interbank. As could be expected, doctors by the dozens jumped in—they can always be found on the autopsy report for a scam. The same for lawyers. Two lawyers who lost big were Orange County's Pat Duffy, who later filed one of the major suits against Bache (a suit since folded into another suit), and San Diego's Gary Aguirre (the brother of Michael Aguirre, the lawyer who filed one of the other major suits against Dominelli's associates).

In many respects J. David was a family adventure: Among the investors were many J. David insiders and their spouses, relatives, and friends. The officials with substantial stakes included Mark Yarry, Richard Colabella, Norman Nouskajian, lawyer Mike Clark, Robert Kritzik, and salesman John Brockington. And there were relatives of Dominelli, Hoover, Ted Pulaski, salesman Robert Smith, Mark Yarry, Asher Schapiro, Robert Kritzik, and others.

Indeed, when a skeptic outside the company would challenge the salespeople about the fantastic returns from J. David, they would frequently mention that their own families were in interbank. "Would I put my mother in it if I were worried about the safety?" one salesman said several times. After the collapse many insiders cited their relatives' investments as proof that they were not aware of the shenanigans going on inside. (This is standard practice in such scams: Charles Ponzi put his wife and her relatives into his scheme.)

Gaining respectability through the politicians, the professionals, and Hoover, and buoyed by the aggressive salesforce and his subterranean ploys, Dominelli took in $200 million that investors believed was going into the foreign currency program. The bulk of the money came in from late 1982 to early 1984. Much of it was withdrawn with fat profits by investors—but those in the game at the end lost $80 million.

Most foreign currency investors were told that only half of their funds would be at risk, and that the balance would go into low-risk short-term paper, such as Treasury bills. Dominelli also stressed that he would take profits quickly and not gamble for the big killing, and that he wouldn't lose more than one percent of a portfolio on any given trade. Thus, Dominelli was telling investors that he took a conservative approach to one of the gamiest markets in the world. The sorry truth is that he did very little trading, direct or indirect, conservative or otherwise, in the foreign exchange market.

But investors didn't know that.

During booming 1983 the J. David family was a happy one. "The business was the center of their lives. Nancy wanted everybody to be happy and to know that she was the queen bee," recalls a former vice-president. And why wouldn't people be happy? The brokers were making unreasonably high commissions. Other employees were vastly overpaid, particularly in light of the perquisites, such as automobiles, they were receiving.

There was, of course, a great deal of concern about the chaos visible all about. However, George Mitrovich helped calm things by explaining that J. David wasn't really chaotic: It was merely "unstructured." It was the modern way to manage. Mitrovich also didn't worry about the cynicism in the community and Dominelli's refusal to communicate with the press. Such things created a useful "mystique," Mitrovich argued.

There *was* a mystique. J. David investors were ecstatic.

They were laughing at the establishment fuddy-duddies who said it couldn't be done. In certain circles the person on the J. David payroll was considered a pioneer, a revolutionary, working for a company that was tearing down all the hoary inhibitions of the past. As the money poured in, it appeared that 1983 would be a magnificent year in La Jolla.

But the euphoric J. David employees had no way of knowing that very dark clouds were forming in Great Britain.

Because of its banking prestige, Great Britain played a key marketing role in the J. David interbank scheme. When an investor put money in interbank, he or she would write a check to J. David Banking. Dominelli's secretary would then tell the investor that the check would be zipped by courier to J. David Banking's London office.

Soon the investor would get a thank-you note from the London office, with the amount of the investment denominated in the British pound, not the U.S. dollar. The check would often be endorsed by some worker in the London office, not by a La Jolla employee, because J. David was trying to keep up the charade that its Montserrat "bank" did no business in California. Investors' monthly statements would also come from London.

Before pulling his money out, the cynical Oklahoma investor, who had been told by a J. David salesman that the firm had a "fully licensed English bank," took a trip to London to take a look at the edifice. "It was a hole in the wall in a lower-middle-class office building in a poor neighborhood," he found.

Similarly, a La Jolla precious metals dealer with important connections in Great Britain had been assaulted by

Dominelli's warriors for some time. Finally he had a friend check out the J. David Banking office. "It's a postage stamp, a brass-plater," said the friend. "Don't touch it."

Hearing such negative reaction, Dominelli then opened a small office in the elegant Plantation House on Fenchurch Street in the heart of the financial district, not far from the Old Lady of Threadneedle Street, the Bank of England.

The cynical Oklahoman went back to London again in early 1983. He had long since closed out his investment, but he was doing detective work just for sport. "That Fenchurch Street office was really nothing more than a reception area with two receptionists. Behind that facade, it was mostly bare."

Just as he had done in the U.S., the Oklahoman took his case to the authorities. He told the whole story to two senior investigators for the Bank of England. They listened carefully and took notes, but said that they really didn't have jurisdiction in the case. They suggested he contact Michael Gillard, a noted British financial journalist. He did. Gillard was fascinated.

At the time in London, the J. David strategy was to have a high profile. Captain Money started behaving uncharacteristically gregariously—just like his Golden Girl. He wined and dined Mark Thatcher, Prime Minister Margaret Thatcher's flamboyant and controversial son. Mark had heard about Dominelli's sponsorship of the British-based Fitzpatrick auto racing team and was eager to get in on the action.

Dominelli apparently didn't understand what it was like to be in the British spotlight. Gillard, who writes bitingly for *Private Eye* and the *London Observer*, got wind of the tête-à-tête and started doing more research into this American parvenu with the fantastic trading record. "The J. David organisation operates out of La Jolla near San Diego," he wrote, "and specialises in currency and commodity dealing. It claims regular profits on the unpredictable foreign exchanges of 40 percent to 50 percent. Such claims have been looked at askance by currency traders in Britain. Even more so as Principal Jerry (David) Dominelli reckons rarely to have a losing month."

Gillard quoted British foreign currency traders as saying, "I would not even dream of making profits like that." Another told Gillard, "It means being so astute as to be unbelievable." And a third simply declared, "It sounds like a hoax."

The Bank of England decided to have a look at J. David Banking. After its probe it issued a cease and desist order: J. David Banking would have to drop the term "banking" from its title. "That is a very specific title which is only granted by the Bank of England after close scrutiny of a company's assets and operations," says Bank of England spokesman Nigel Falls. J. David Banking was told it could not engage in any banking activities or use names such as "bank," "banking," "trust," "trust company," or any word connoting banking.

Dominelli was undeterred. He turned to a subsidiary, J. David International, which had initially been set up to operate as a full-service financial operation, selling commodities, stocks, bonds, insurance, and the like. J. David International, incorporated in the U.K. without benefit or assistance of counsel, would now take over the functions of the former J. David Banking. J. David could now tell the British that J. David Banking had no employees in the U.K.

The British remained skeptical. Twice J. David International tried to get a listing on the London International Financial Futures Exchange (LIFFE), and twice it was turned down, even though Dominelli had hired the most expensive British barristers through Rogers & Wells to argue its case, and even though San Diego Mayor Hedgecock had sent a glowing recommendation. Dominelli so desperately wanted LIFFE membership that in May 1983 he considered permitting an English accounting firm to audit his interbank fund for the first time. But Dominelli gave the accountant specific instructions: "You are requested and authorized to issue an opinion letter stating that . . . the money from new investors is not being used in any way to make distributions of cash to earlier investors." In other words, Dominelli authorized the accountant to affirm that J. David was not running a Ponzi scheme. The audit was never performed.

The first LIFFE rejection was in July 1982, just before the exchange opened, and the second was in late 1983. The second time, J. David International tried to buy an existing seat for $65,000, but was rebuffed. The LIFFE won't say why it rejected J. David, but there can be three reasons: lack of a sound reputation, lack of sufficient or relevant experience in the business, or inadequate net worth.

"I believe that the Bank of England intervened in keeping J. David from getting that LIFFE seat," says John Shockey of the Comptroller of the Currency, echoing a view that many others hold.

(The British refusal to grant the LIFFE seat did not, by the way, stop Dominelli from claiming in a 1983 offering for his Vacuum Marketing and Research Associates partnership that he actually *had* the seat.)

Scotland Yard, too, examined J. David, according to Yard spokesman Nick Jordan. And fraud inspectors for the City of London Police investigated allegations that J. David was illegally accepting bank deposits, had failed to register as a bank, and was "exaggerating investment potential" through its claim that investors were making 40 to 50 percent annually on their money in a virtually uninterrupted monthly stream. And the British Commonwealth Office, which supervises commercial operations in British crown colonies, including Montserrat, probed whether J. David was fraudulently claiming that its London J. David Banking branch was a British-licensed bank. Neither the police nor the Commonwealth office came up with conclusive proof of illegal activity, but it's obvious that the British agencies kept watching the situation.

One high-level British official, refusing to disclose his name or even his agency, comments, "Let's just say that we have been aware of the J. David situation for quite some time."

Clearly, the Bank of England was the heavyweight. Ironically, it had entered the picture partly at J. David's invitation. In 1982 and 1983 Dominelli tried to get his Class B Montserrat banking license (essentially, a license for a brass plate) upgraded to a Class A license, which would permit the "bank" to take deposits. If he got the Class A license, he would then attempt to convince British banking authorities to issue J. David International a "representative office" license (still a long way from a full banking license). In a memo to Nouskajian in early 1983, J. David's in-house counsel said that British banking authorities were "more or less favorably disposed" to considering an application for this "representative office" license.

According to a former J. David employee in the London office, as well as some former La Jolla employees and investors, the showdown came in October 1983. The Bank of England wrote J. David and told it to prepare to open its books. The Bank of England refuses to say whether it did this, and a few Britishers doubt that it happened. However, Michael Aguirre theorizes that the Bank of England had reason to believe that J. David was illegally accepting deposits, "and it wanted to take a look and see." Or, perhaps, it was making an investigation related to the attempt to get a "representative office" license.

In any case, according to the story by the former London employee, Yarry panicked when he got the Bank of England notification. He and his two assistants, Warwick Salvage and William Hole (Yarry's brother-in-law), huddled. Yarry decided to move the records—and much of the rest of the office—to a London hotel. After that, plans were made to transfer J. David from London to Lugano, Switzerland.

It was an urgently necessary move, because J. David's foreign currency operation could never have withstood a competent audit. But it would turn out to be a fatal move.

In just a few months, London, Lugano, and Montserrat would dominate the rumor mill in San Diego. Later, they would dominate the news. George Mitrovich was prepared. Shaking his head, radiating erudition, he explained the initial criticism patronizingly. "It's unfortunate that very few Southern Californians really understand the world of foreign currency trading."

7

The Run Begins

In late 1983 things in Great Britain were going *down*, but back in La Jolla, J. David had plans to go *up*—upmarket, upscale.

J. David was preparing to offer a foreign exchange trading account with a minimum $2 million investment. An investor in the fund, to be administered by J. David International Arbitrage, Ltd., would be required to have a minimum net worth of $1 million; the investment would be made largely with borrowed funds.

And J. David was moving *up* geographically: This fund would be based in Bermuda, rather than Montserrat.

Attorney Norman Nouskajian prepared a very official-appearing offering document. Of course, a couple of things remained the same. Said the offering, "The accounts have not been registered under either the United States Banking Acts, Securities Act of 1933, or under the laws of any other State, country or jurisdiction." And, it added, "No statement or advice is given by the Company regarding the tax consequences under the laws of the Account holder's domicile or residence which will result from Account transactions."

The offering document was worded conservatively, but the J. David salespeople were making wild claims. "They were talking about doubling your money in sixty days," says the Oklahoma investor, who correctly sensed that J. David was getting desperate for cash inflow.

In London, the plan to move J. David to Switzerland was going forward. Yarry, who had worked the European circuit for years, was calling the signals. It was decided that a "trust" would be set up in Switzerland to administer the interbank investments. The word "trust" was important. Trusts are supposed to be neutral parties, working on behalf of customers at an arm's length from the group running an investment operation. However, J. David established a "trust," not a trust. Mark Yarry simply resigned as head of J. David Banking and became head of the "trust," which was coyly named Threadneedle Trust Services, S.A. and was to be based in Lugano, near the Italian border.

With the move Dominelli hoped to make a silk purse out of a sow's ear. He planned to play up the trust aspect, not letting on that it was set up only because J. David was on the lam out of Britain.

First National Bank, for one, was impressed. In an internal memo, Thomas LaHay wrote, "Jerry hopes that once and for all this will legitimize their operation in the eyes of local critics." But Dominelli had apparently misled LaHay into believing that Mark Yarry would be "the intermediary between J. David and the trust." LaHay had not been told that Yarry was chief executive in charge of the trust.

The Lugano maneuver notwithstanding, First National was getting queasy about J. David. Bank memoranda show that as early as August 1983 J. David had overdrawn its account by $328,000. The bank loaned J. David the money to cover the amount. But Yarry considered the interest on the loan a nuisance charge and threatened to move the account. The bank's president, Edward G. Cunningham, noted in a memo, "He [Yarry] finally understood that overdraft approvals constituted unsecured loans. I asked him if he really believed that they could move their account relationship and find a bank that would loan them $400,000 as we did this week. We particularly were not happy when we were told that the money was on its way and it did not arrive."

There were other problems in mid-1983. Some trading equipment went down, but Dominelli wouldn't get it repaired. "Jerry was often late with bills. The word was that Jerry wanted to use other people's money," recalls Robert Mengar. By fall some suppliers were not being paid. Some employees close to the throne were asked if they would take deferred compensation arrangements. And, employees found out later, Dominelli started missing payments on their Blue Cross coverage in the late fall of 1983.

J. David personnel were vaguely cognizant of the environment changing for the worse. "I came back from Europe the first week in September. I knew something was wrong, just the way people were acting. Jerry was reported to have just taken a hell of a hit [a big loss in the foreign currency market]," says Mengar. Obviously, Dominelli—great actor though he was—couldn't completely conceal his worries. But he knew how to mask that frown on his face in front of employees: He was blaming it on his trading record (although he was doing almost no trading). He continued to tell *customers* they were making fat monthly returns.

The public facade never cracked. If anything, Captain Money and the Golden Girl were spending money more rapidly and conspicuously than ever. In November Hoover began sporting a Bulgari emerald ring worth $40,000. "Isn't it wonderful? It's my engagement ring!" she told Sandra Kritzik. In mid-December Dominelli and Hoover threw a big party for the triathletes and another for the children of employees.

But back at the office, toward the end of December, some checks started to bounce. Salesmen faced infuriated investors who couldn't cash their J. David checks. Dominelli took to delaying vendors' payments across the board. In late December J. David still had not paid its rent to a local real estate firm. "I wrote letters and called the secretary several times," remembers Linda Dowley, an agent at William Donovan and Co. "She always said it would be coming. Finally, my boss said, 'Does Dominelli know about this? See if he knows what's going on there.' I called and asked the secretary if I could speak with Mr. Dominelli. She asked why. I said I wanted to be sure he knew that his company was not paying bills. She said, 'You can be certain that Mr. Dominelli knows of our cash-flow problem.'"

Word of similar happenings spread throughout San Diego.

Still, many employees were not alarmed. They were aware company bookkeeping had always been chaotic. Perhaps, they said, the sloppiness was just becoming known in the community.

Only a handful of employees knew that Jerry David Dominelli was frantically trying to raise money. "Guess who wants to borrow money? Jerry Dominelli, the guy who *has* all the money," said Robert Kritzik to his wife, Sandra, in mid-December.

Dominelli had told Kritzik that he was trying to buy Commodity Monitors, a San Diego-based statistical firm that Nancy wanted. "We suggested that he borrow from the J. David [interbank] fund," says Kritzik. But Dominelli replied he would rather not. Kritzik did not get suspicious.

Dominelli then tried to borrow several million dollars from Allen Glick, the La Jollan who had owned the controversial casinos in Las Vegas. Glick had two of his financial lieutenants look at the Commodity Monitors deal.

"Jerry, we're not brokers. If we were to get involved, we'd want to get in as owners," Glick's lieutenants told him. They turned it down. (Glick, who did not attend the meeting, later went to a Hoover-Dominelli party in Rancho Santa Fe. "It was a little strained," recalls Kritzik.)

Dominelli called more friends to try to raise money on the grounds that he wanted to buy Commodity Monitors. He had little luck.

In December employees and good customers began pulling money out of interbank. Among those to withdraw funds were Yarry and his relatives; Richard Colabella; lawyer Maurile Tremblay and his firm, Wiles, Circuit & Tremblay; trading adviser William Griffo; John Brockington; members of Pulaski's family; Jay Gordon of Teachersworth Services; Dominelli's close friend William Galt, a major investor; Axelrod's Transatlantic Bancorp; and Richard Mangiarelli, an ex-Marine and ex–San Diego

Charger football player who was a very large investor and a good friend of Dominelli's.

"I suspected something and was trying to get my customers diversified. I was recommending they take money out and get into something else. One pulled out $750,000 and Jerry came to me to ask if I could do anything about it," says a former interbank salesman.

But the annual yearend party at the elegant Hotel del Coronado was more extravagant than usual. Hoover, radiant, sparkled her way around the guests. Even Dominelli smiled occasionally. A senior financial officer, though, incredulously eyed the waiters in tuxedos liberally pouring champagne. He was aware that payments to suppliers were being delayed. "It was too unreal. We had missed the premium payment for health insurance and were having this grand ball at the Hotel del. I got to thinking that it's the *Titanic*. Here we are dining on filet mignon and we're sinking."

Another employee remembers saying to himself, "This will be the last J. David party I'll ever attend." But to this day he claims he didn't have anything specific to go on.

And some who had been closest to Dominelli were experiencing a dawning: They were recalling Dominelli's words and actions of the past, putting them together, and coming up with frighteningly ugly pictures. "Dominelli is a pathological liar," said Nouskajian to Robert Kritzik. Shortly Nouskajian would be pulling his own money out of interbank.

In early January uneasy people on both the inside and the outside were waiting for some information on what was happening. Inadvertently Dominelli gave the first clue. He sent the following letter to interbank clients:

EFFECTIVE JANUARY 9, 1984

Dear Client:

In our review of current procedures in the operation of your Interbank account, we have decided to implement a series of changes which we believe is in our mutual interest.

We have entered into an arrangement with Threadneedle Trust Services, S.A., a fiduciary trustee in Switzerland, to open individual trust accounts for all our clients. Threadneedle Trust Services is supervised under strict Swiss regulations and will act on your behalf. You will in the future be receiving your monthly statement direct from the trust company. They will, as is required by Swiss Law, review all transactions made in your account. You will receive an annual audited statement from the Trustee.

We have negotiated on your behalf a fee for trust services in the amount of Five Hundred U.S. Dollars per annum payable for each account in advance.

Your funds will continue to be managed in the Foreign Exchange Market as in the past by J. David & Company as an advisor to the trust company.

There will be a change in Management fees as of April 1, 1984. Your account will be charged one percent per month of funds under management instead of the twenty percent incentive fee. This is the first change in our basic management charge since the inception of Interbank trading. It is our expectation that this change will additionally benefit each of our clients.

DEPOSITS AND WITHDRAWALS FROM TRUST ACCOUNTS

All deposits to your trust account should be made payable to Threadneedle Trust Services, S.A. Client Trust Account, by Cashiers Check or Wire Transfer, and sent directly to Privat Kredit Bank, V. Pretorio 22, 6901 Lugano, Switzerland. It is absolutely essential that you include your name and account number when making deposits. Neither the trust company or the bank will be responsible for deposits received without this information. Personal checks take up to two weeks to clear and will be credited only upon receipt of good funds at the bank in Lugano.

Withdrawals from your trust account can be made by calling (011 41 91) 23 16 53 between the hours of six a.m. and nine a.m. Pacific Time. You must give your name and account number for the withdrawal to be processed. Allow ten business days for all withdrawals, which will be sent directly to you by bankers draft through Privat Kredit Bank. The J. David office in La Jolla cannot under any circumstances accept deposits or withdrawals to your account.

Shortly, you will be receiving from Threadneedle new custodial and management agreements to be executed and returned to them for processing. Threadneedle Trust Services offers many other services to its clients and will be sending you information on these activities.

We look forward to another prosperous year and thank you for your continued support and confidence.

The Board of Directors
J. DAVID BANKING COMPANY, LTD.

To those in the know, Dominelli was making some significant moves. For the first time, the interbank fund would be audited, albeit by a Swiss company, and customers would be receiving an annual audited statement. And deposits would no longer be taken in La Jolla—a signal that J. David was planning to do what it was telling the California Department of Banking it was already doing.

But Dominelli was trying to extract a hefty price for these changes. There was the $500 annual trust assessment. Much more importantly, investors would be paying a compounded 13 percent a year on their *total balance* rather than 20 percent on that year's profits. As a San Diegan observed, "That would be a huge increase. And a 13 percent annual fee is exceedingly high—almost unheard of."

At the time Dominelli insisted that the fee change would only diminish customers' profits by 10 percent. The increase, he said, was necessary for "planning purposes." But he admitted the letter had boomeranged: "We got a very negative response. People thought we were abandoning them."

Within a few days customers received the trust material from Threadneedle. San Diego lawyer Norman J. Elliott, looking over the proposed trust agreement for a client, commented, "There is never an indication who the people [constituting Threadneedle] are." If there is no separation between Threadneedle and J. David, "that destroys the concept of a trust," Elliott said. He advised his client to get away from J. David in a hurry. Others in the community expressed their cynicism, but nobody knew that the doubts were absolutely on target: J. David and the "trust" were one and the same.

The withdrawals escalated—and once again, they were being made largely by employees or investors who were very close to employees. It was clearly an inside run. Dominelli tried to offset the hemorrhaging by not paying his bills.

Money that was coming in was "turning right around and going out," says Kenneth Poovey, a San Diego lawyer who was called in by suspicious investors to check out the situation in late January. Dominelli began paying his money-finders as much as 20 percent in a frantic effort to bring in more money.

One time-tested way to attract more money is to make more money for clients. Thus, Dominelli reported to investors that they had made a smashing 7 percent in January. Star salesman Pulaski got the news while talking on the phone long-distance with Dominelli. "Seven percent?! Great! Fantastic!" Pulaski yelled. One investor who saw the performance considers it exculpatory evidence: Pulaski couldn't have known what Dominelli was doing.

Dominelli's money-raising strategies only intensified some insiders' skepticism. The restiveness was getting feverish.

To appease critics, Dominelli offered the use of one of his jets for an investor "fact-finding trip" to Lugano. On the trip were investor Richard Rosenblatt and two colleagues, Pulaski and some other insiders, and a couple of potential investors. Rosenblatt stopped in London to see if Lloyd's of London might be able to insure the J. David operation. The rest went on to Lugano to talk with Threadneedle and Privat Kredit Bank. They also spoke with lawyer Mike Clark, who was there setting up Threadneedle. Despite solemn assurances from the Swiss, they were more upset than ever on finding that Threadneedle was headed by Mark Yarry. One of the persons who made the trip went to the FBI when he returned to San Diego.

Among themselves, employees whispered, Was the money there? Nouskajian and Clark tried to persuade the doubters that it was. Clark had seen it, he claimed.

Journalists began hearing the rumors in January. Financial writers for the major papers read in San Diego—the *Union*, the *Tribune*, the *Los Angeles Times*, and the *Daily Transcript*—had been dubious about Dominelli's activities for some time. (The stories on J. David that ran in late 1982 were filled with loaded expressions, such as "the elusive J. David" and "raised eyebrows.") Fred Muir, who had done the 1982 *Union* story and had talked extensively with the cynical Oklahoma investor and others, was frustrated that he hadn't been able to get the heart of the story into print. But at the time he just did not have enough substantive material to satisfy the newspaper's lawyers and senior editors.

Attempts by several papers to obtain interviews with Dominelli in late January were unsuccessful. A representative of the *Transcript* had sat outside Dominelli's office on two different days.

Since Muir had just left the *Union* for the *Wall Street Journal*, the Dominelli story fell to me as the *Union* financial editor. I called Walter Shaw, whom I knew and who had just come aboard as president of J. David Securities. I was surprised when I was told to drop in the next day for an interview. Even though Dominelli had consistently refused all requests to be photographed, I was also told that it was OK to bring a photographer.

The next afternoon, January 26, I showed up with the photographer. There had been a mix-up: Dominelli wouldn't let his picture be taken. But Mitrovich permitted the photographer to shoot Dominelli's desk, with piles of newspapers strewn all around.

I interviewed Dominelli for three hours. He admitted that some of the rumors were true: Checks were bouncing, investors couldn't get their money out as fast as they formerly could, and he would have to make personnel slashes. For a reason no one understands, he also said that there was only $35 million to $40 million in interbank, even though his top employees had been told there was four times that much. (Soon he would be telling a bankruptcy trustee that he had had $150 million in the fund and $25 million had been withdrawn in the December–January run.)

In the interview Dominelli claimed that the bouncing checks resulted from an administrative snafu related to the move from London to Lugano. He had explanations of varying plausibility for his other problems. He told me some big lies, such as that he was about to make a major acquisition and had purchased a seat on the New York Stock Exchange. He gave me a copy of the letter he had sent to investors and admitted that it had caused a ruckus.

He also gave me a new letter that was about to go out. It recanted the 13-percent-a-year charge on the total balance. The old 20-percent-of-profits fee would remain intact "for the foreseeable future." And the Threadneedle operation would be optional. The letter now identified Privat Kredit Bank as "a large private bank." (In truth, it is a tiny bank.) And the letter defended the move to Switzerland, noting that the Lugano bankers and lawyers "are people of the highest quality and reputation."

I returned to my office feeling little short of triumphant. I had gone into the interview without proof of the bounced checks. I had been armed only with hearsay and had not expected Dominelli to confess. Nor had I expected him to admit that people could not get their money out on time and that he would be slashing personnel. For competitive reasons we decided to run the story the next day and not hold it to check some of Dominelli's explanations. The managing editor, city editor, house lawyer, and I all agreed that the story should be completely objective, and it was.

It related the problems, but gave Dominelli's explanations. The accompanying photograph of Dominelli's paper-strewn office—without Dominelli—was, in retrospect, the best bit of interpretative graphic journalism the paper had done in years. The story became identified as "the empty chair story."

On the day it appeared, Dominelli said that the story was "objective." Later he blamed it for the deluge. Mitrovich didn't like the emphasis and said he would have selected different words in some cases. The sales personnel were livid: Their phones were ringing off the hook. They sensed the worst. The run had become an avalanche.

The next week Mark Yarry left La Jolla for Switzerland, where he had been spending most of his time setting up the Threadneedle "trust." "I was on my way to Switzerland and I made a routine phone call [back to La Jolla] from the East. Rumors were circulating that I was leaving the country with the money," related Yarry later in an interview with me. Upset, he caught a flight back to California and appeared in the J. David office the following day to calm employees.

But there was no calming them. Lines of irate investors were outside Dominelli's office. One was waving a gun. One handicapped investor stood there for eight hours. As more and more checks bounced, Dominelli wrote cashier's checks to cover them. Plaintive letters and notes poured in: People desperately wanted to close their accounts.

Many called Lugano, as they had been told to do, and were informed there was no money there. Dominelli had not yet admitted that the Threadneedle "trust" had not in fact been set up.

One woman requested her money several times over

eleven days. Finally her lawyer wrote, "All these requests, made by numerous telephone calls to your La Jolla office and Lugano, have been met with lies and evasions."

Judge Bianchini left his card. A secretary made the notation: "Life savings." Then she underlined the words, "is here."

Several investors said they needed the money urgently for deals they had in escrow. One lamented he had "already used the money to live on." He was "real scared," noted the secretary. Lawyers threatened legal action, including the institution of voluntary bankruptcy proceedings.

The squeakiest wheels were getting the grease. Under Dominelli's instructions secretaries put certain people on the "critical list," and they got their funds first.

While people waited in lines outside his office, Dominelli was doing two things: approving the disbursement of checks to certain clients and frenetically trying to raise money. On January 24 he borrowed $2.26 million from four investors in Orange County and San Francisco. They, too, had been told the money was for the purchase of Commodity Monitors. But the money was paid out to investors. These and other loans had maturities of only a few days, and some of the lenders, upon being turned down for payment, joined the investors in line.

M. Larry Lawrence, former chairman of the California Democratic Party, chief executive of the Hotel del Coronado, and a partner with Dominelli in the takeover of Yuba Natural Resources, loaned him $1 million, to be repaid two days later. Dominelli offered two of his jets as collateral. As soon as Lawrence gave him the money, it went right out to investors. Dominelli then directed that one of the airplanes be flown to Switzerland, telling Lawrence he would not return it to the U.S. unless he received additional cash. Lawrence sued to get the airplane—and a fistfight broke out when Lawrence's agents tried to take the plane away from Dominelli's crew in Switzerland.

But a fistfight in a foreign land would be the least of Dominelli's problems. Back home, a J. David insider, on the job just three weeks, had figured out the entire scheme. He was Nicholas F. Coscia, a former SEC attorney, who had been brought in, he was told, to assure J. David's compliance with state and federal laws. Immediately he discovered that J. David attorneys Norman Nouskajian and Mike Clark were reluctant to give him any information. Clark called Coscia into his office and told him that he (Coscia) had a "personality conflict with everybody there" and that he (Clark) would try to get him fired. Clark denies that account, but admits he talked with Dominelli about Coscia.

"I was faced with extreme resistance to my presence," says Coscia. "They denied me access, tried to block me in the hope of keeping me out. They didn't feel they could trust me with what they considered to be sensitive information." The stumbling block was interbank.

It was a difficult time for Coscia. He had left an excellent job with the SEC and, he soon discovered, had taken employment with a firm pulling off a monstrous Ponzi scheme. One lawyer who sat in with him on meetings during that period observed, "He was very nervous, said little. He must have been pissing in his pants."

Coscia wasted no time. On February 9 he wrote a letter to William P. Rogers, head of Rogers & Wells (Nouskajian's firm), and to Gary H. Wiles, head of Wiles, Circuit &

Tremblay (Clark's firm). He also sent a copy to Jerry Boltz, the former head of the Los Angeles office of the SEC, who was then working for the Los Angeles office of Rogers & Wells. Rogers and Boltz were thoroughly familiar with securities law.

J. David "may be selling unregistered securities in the form of investment contracts," Coscia stated and then elaborated on some of the specifics: J. David's salesmen solicit individuals to invest in a pool of funds domiciled overseas. The investors sign an agreement calling for Dominelli to trade their money at his discretion. Investments as small as $10,000 are put into the fund, despite the professed $50,000 minimum, and the customers deposit money into and withdraw money from the fund through the company headquarters in La Jolla.

The "company may be an unregistered investment company and an unregistered investment adviser," Coscia went on, noting that monies not invested in the fund were invested in Eurodollar certificates of deposit, municipal bonds, and other paper and were redeemable on demand. Further, J. David "may be an unregistered broker-dealer and [the] salesmen unregistered representatives," wrote Coscia.

And finally, Coscia's most damning charge: "[The] monies raised for the fund may have been completely dissipated." He explained how investors were complaining that they could not get their money out. "I have been unable for two weeks to independently verify whether or not any investor monies remain in the fund," Coscia said. Insiders had told him there was $140 million in the pool, but he could not get cooperation from others on the matter.

"When I informed Nouskajian that I was unable to verify the amount of money in the fund, he indicated that he had also been unable to make any such verification because that was something Dominelli had always kept to himself," wrote Coscia. Clark and Don McVay, a former Rogers & Wells attorney working on the payroll of J. David, had refused to discuss the matter, according to the letter. "When Clark returned from Switzerland, I asked him whether he had been able to verify the amount of investor monies on deposit with the fund in Switzerland. He informed me he would provide me with no such information because that matter was exclusively between him and Dominelli."

Almost immediately, Rogers & Wells and Wiles, Circuit & Tremblay ended their relationships with Dominelli, who would soon be headed into bankruptcy court—and a criminal grand jury hearing—without legal representation.

And Coscia wasn't alone: An outsider had the scam pegged, too. San Diego lawyer Kenneth Poovey had been hired by a number of investors to determine what was going on, to find out if J. David was a Ponzi scheme and if there was any money left. Poovey assembled a team of experts, and over a two-week period they interviewed more than one hundred investors and employees, as well as interbank professionals and others on the outside.

They concluded that Dominelli was clearly running a Ponzi scheme. He had been spending the money as fast as it came in. Interbank professionals didn't know Dominelli: It was obvious he had done very little actual trading from the beginning with the money he was taking in. Poovey checked out the banks where Dominelli allegedly had money and learned there was very little in them.

Assuming that there had been no trading losses (because there had been little trading), Poovey calculated that

Dominelli had taken in $60 million to $80 million from investors. Then his team started figuring Dominelli's expenses. Recalls Poovey, "Airplanes. Estate. Condominiums. Racehorses. Triathletes team. Porsche racing team. Jewelry—that was significant. Negative cash flow in the operation . . . this was $1 million to $1.25 million a month. Bonuses and huge commissions for brokers. Leasehold improvements [the offices]. The gold mine [Dominelli's stake in Yuba]." And some investors had pulled their money out with huge profits.

Poovey added up the expenditures, subtracted them from the money taken in, and concluded that Dominelli might have $10 million left.

Some of Poovey's clients were J. David employees, who shared the findings with colleagues. Some of them tried to figure how the supposedly remaining $10 million could be distributed to investors and the whole debacle kept out of bankruptcy court. In any bankruptcy, lawyers wind up with a significant part of the assets, and investors wanted to avoid that.

Nouskajian and Hoover, according to several insiders, went to Dominelli and told him that he could simply liquidate the company and distribute whatever was left to the investors. Some insiders who were by this time convinced that Dominelli had illegally spent the money tried to devise a way for him to claim that he lost it trading—tell investors the game was over and then distribute the remaining funds. But Dominelli was buying none of the suggestions. He wanted to keep going.

That's because he knew—or at least was almost sure— that he didn't have $10 million.

First National Bank was first to pull the plug. In the late

fall it had gotten progressively more disturbed by constant overdrafts. To cover the situation, First National agreed to issue J. David a line of credit secured by a $1 million certificate of deposit. Thomas LaHay and Chris Kalabokes agreed that the line of credit should be meted out gingerly. "It would be too tempting for Jerry Dominelli and Mark [Yarry] to utilize the full $1 million if it were available," said LaHay in a First National memo. An $800,000 line of credit was arranged, but it never went into effect, because J. David never came up with the $1 million certificate of deposit. The bank began bouncing checks in December.

In late December LaHay talked with Dominelli and was assured that J. David would purchase $3 million in time deposits from First National no later than January 5, 1984. Nothing happened.

Dominelli promised to wire additional money from Lugano. In early January, as the bank continued to bounce checks, LaHay went to La Jolla to speak with Dominelli once more. "I again related our concern over the way the accounts were being handled and that we could not continue the relationship in its present status. Dominelli assured me again that the situation was now under control and that we would have anywhere between $2 million and $4 million wired into the bank before the end of this week," LaHay wrote in a memo.

The money never came. On January 12 LaHay sent Dominelli a stiff note threatening to close the account in four days. The same day he told Kalabokes that First National wouldn't honor payroll checks on Group J. David accounts unless the funds were there.

Then some money (from new investors) came into the

account and First National kept it open. Dominelli autho-
rized Yarry to go to Swiss Bank Corp. in Geneva and bring
$10 million in a draft or a certified check to First National.
But Yarry developed an eye infection, and on January 30
Dominelli said that the courier would be attorney Mike
Clark.

Throughout the February 4–5 weekend, LaHay waited
for a call from Dominelli that the money had come. On
Monday, February 6, Dominelli explained that Clark's law
firm partners objected to his being the courier. Dominelli
promised that the money would be wire-transferred to First
National. It never was, and later that day First National
closed the account. At the time First National had no way
of knowing that the reason $10 million never came from
Swiss Bank Corp. was that there was a total of $32,000 in
the account.

By now J. David was the talk of San Diego. People were
predicting an imminent collapse. Mitrovich, however, had
an explanation: A deadly sin had raised its ugly head. Of
those spreading rumors, Mitrovich declared, "There are a
great number of people who are very envious of Jerry
Dominelli."

8

The Ship Hits an Iceberg.
Something Hits the Fan, Too

It's not surprising that the senior financial officer viewing the merriment at the J. David yearend party was put in mind of the *Titanic*. Corporate financial executives and Wall Street officers are forever using analogies tied to the disaster. An inept chief executive officer is said to be the "captain of the *Titanic*." A board of directors making cosmetic changes at a company headed for catastrophe is "rearranging the deck chairs on the *Titanic*." A pending problem is "that iceberg ahead."

Anyone foreseeing a corporate failure should read up on the *Titanic*. It provides poignant lessons in human behavior: the passengers' giddiness, their obliviousness to looming disaster; the crew's overconfidence, its utter certainty that the ship was unsinkable. But most of all, the disaster illustrates the ugly tenacity of the self-preservation instinct—the people in the lifeboats hysterically refusing to let others aboard, smashing them over the head with oars to keep them from scrambling onto the rafts, shoving them back into the icy water to die.

People act the same way in the days leading up to a bankruptcy. The ship is going down. There aren't enough life rafts. Some will make it to shore and others won't. You have to make it, and to hell with the others.

Throughout almost the entire history of J. David, investors were actuated by only one emotion: greed. In the last days, there was a new monomania: survival. Once the news of bounced checks and bounced employees, unpaid suppliers and unpaid investors, hit the streets, the run was on and the oars were flying.

In most corporate collapses, the debtor holds the high card: the threat of bankruptcy. Lenders and suppliers consider bankruptcy the worst way to recover their funds.

Attorney Kenneth Poovey, hired by a group of investors, was hoping to keep the matter out of bankruptcy court. So were lawyers representing some other investors. But in this case Dominelli wasn't threatening to play his high card: He didn't want bankruptcy. After all, any serious court action—a bankruptcy or, say, divorce proceedings by his estranged wife—could force him to open his books, and if they revealed that he had been running a Ponzi scheme and had swindled tens of millions out of investors, that alone would be enough to send him to jail.

Creditors in the J. David case weren't quite as reluctant as usual to push for bankruptcy. There was the $10 million bond from Chubb. There were visible assets, such as the ornate corporate headquarters in La Jolla, that had some value. There were all those homes and cars and fancy furs, although the homes were known to be highly leveraged.

And there were some special mare's nests in J. David that a court of law might have to clean up—the Montserrat-based "bank," for example.

Nonbankruptcy liquidation seemed most unlikely. Generally, in such a liquidation, three conditions must be met: The debtor must be honest and cooperative, the business must be relatively simple, and the records must be complete. J. David failed on all counts. And many investors overcome an initial aversion to bankruptcy because they know they can often recoup part of their money by bringing action against law, accounting, and brokerage firms that provide services to the malefactors and may carry heavy insurance for such contingencies. These "deep pockets" often cave in and ante up, partly because of the negative publicity and partly out of fear that in private lawsuits, more documents will be unearthed and more serious wounds opened.

Dominelli hastened his own demise by feeding investor paranoia through his attempts to make side deals with numerous clients in the waning days of J. David. One investor who had been waiting in the halls overheard plans by insiders to transfer $275,000 in cash to someone. A lawyer got wind of a proposed deal and charged, "One of the creditors has made a private deal with Dominelli to refrain from taking action against Dominelli, providing that Dominelli or his entities transfer substantial sums of money to an offshore bank by the end of the week."

Says William C. Starrett II of Newport Beach, a lawyer for Arthur Axelrod, whose Transatlantic Bancorp had raised more than $10 million for interbank, "Dominelli was making promises to herds of people. The people on the outside of these side deals were obviously upset. It appeared everyone was in on some side deal." Dominelli was known to be phoning larger investors constantly. Investors who had not heard from him were hysterical. They feared that what little money existed was being siphoned off to the big boys who could get optimum arrangements—or to organized crime–connected thugs who could threaten to make the *ultimate* arrangement.

In late January and February 1984, as investors and last-minute lenders remonstrated outside his office, hounded him by phone and by wire, and pressured brokers within the organization to intercede on their behalf, Dominelli sensed he was rowing with one oar. Even George Mitrovich perceived an aura of disunion: "I don't know how to characterize what's going on around here. Definitely, it's not normal activity," he said to a reporter on February 9.

Both of San Diego's large establishment law firms—Luce, Forward, Hamilton & Scripps, and Gray, Cary, Ames & Frye—were in the center of the storm. Luce, Forward was representing Thomas DiNoto, the jingle writer who had more than $1 million in interbank. Gray, Cary represented Axelrod.

Luce, Forward prepared a suit charging Dominelli with violation of federal securities and racketeering laws and presented it to Dominelli and his lawyer Maurile Tremblay on February 6. If DiNoto's money did not come through by February 9, the suit would be filed, said the firm. The parties met several times, and Dominelli's lawyers explained that there was a logistic problem moving the money out of Switzerland. "We said to Tremblay that we would accept our client's money wherever it could be legally transferred," says Charles Bird, the Luce, Forward attorney. The firm hired a Swiss law firm to act as intermediary and to help untangle the perceived snarls.

Bird did not know, but he suspected, that the only snarl was that Dominelli had no money in Switzerland. Bird was certainly unaware that at the same time his firm was presenting the suit to Tremblay, First National was closing the J. David checking account because none of the promised money had come from Switzerland. "We knew the relationship was strained, but didn't know it had been terminated," he says, remembering that throughout the negotiations Dominelli frequently referred to his fine standing at First National.

The final meeting involved Dominelli, Tremblay, and Robert Harlan, another of Dominelli's lawyers. "Tremblay told Dominelli that he should not agree to anything he couldn't do, but Dominelli still said he'd sign whatever it took," recalls Bird. But there was one overriding problem: "Dominelli was unable to produce any cash at all," says Bird.

It was deadline day, February 9, and getting toward 4:00 P.M.—time for Bird to stand up, unilaterally adjourn the meeting, and declare the suit would be filed within an hour. As he did so, Harlan warned, "Don't kill the goose that lays the golden eggs!"

Just fifteen minutes later, the suit was filed and the media were alerted. Dominelli made himself scarce, but his cohorts got his side across. Earlier that day, lawyer Nouskajian had told me that "as of 11:40 A.M. on February 9," not a single person entitled to receive money had not been paid. He didn't mention that a month earlier, he had pulled his own money out.

Also on February 9, M. Larry Lawrence said that he had checked out Dominelli with bankers in Paris, New York, Switzerland, Hong Kong, and Chicago and found he had an impeccable reputation. No questions about Dominelli's financial health had arisen except in San Diego, insisted Lawrence, who stated he had a large investment with Dominelli. Rumors of a J. David bankruptcy filing or contemplation were, he contended, totally untrue, and Dominelli was the victim of rumors and newspaper witch-hunting. "The stories have created the problem, not the problem created the stories," explained Lawrence. But he didn't explain that his investment was in the form of a last-minute loan to Dominelli nor that his son had pulled out more than $100,000 several days before.

The evening of the day Bird stalked out of the office and told his associates to file the suit, Dominelli, Hoover, Dominelli's handyman Parin Columna, and several others descended on headquarters with huge green trash bags and stuffed them with critical documents. Columna then stashed the bags at a number of locations in Orange and San Diego counties. And Dominelli and his minions started selling off the automobiles.

They knew they were headed for bankruptcy, and they had to spirit away the evidence and dispose of assets before the trustee took over.

The story of the lawsuit and of First National's cancellation of the banking relationship ran in the *San Diego Union* the next day, a Friday. At J. David it was Black Friday. Lines lengthened, tension heightened.

The biggest showdown was still to come, Dominelli knew. The same week, he had been conducting intense negotiations with Arthur Axelrod of Transatlantic Bancorp, whose investors believed they had $16 million in principal and interest in interbank. Understandably, the anxious investors now wanted their money back.

Axelrod suspected that Dominelli was double-crossing him. In November 1983 Dominelli had agreed to buy Transatlantic (essentially its client list) for $2 million. The $2 million was to be paid in ten installments. In the meantime Axelrod would transfer a $4.7 million investors' reserve account he kept in a Bermuda bank to First National Bank of San Diego, but he would retain sole signatory authority. In January, however, Axelrod discovered that the $4.7 million had never made it into First National. Dominelli had routed the money elsewhere, no doubt to pay off investors. Axelrod was furious, and Dominelli sent him an $800,000 check. It bounced. More fury. Then Dominelli sent several checks totaling $521,000. They bounced, too. Axelrod erupted. In mid-January he and his attorneys huddled with Dominelli. In late January Dominelli tried to pacify Axelrod by boasting that profits that month would be 7 to 13 percent. Dominelli cooed, "We are whole."

But Axelrod wasn't appeased. On the last day of January, he demanded all his funds. He sat in Dominelli's office on Friday, February 3, and on Sunday, February 5. Dominelli promised the money by Monday, the sixth; Axelrod was there waiting for it. Then Dominelli said $4 million would be available, but the balance would come "in a day or two." On the sixth Axelrod got no money at all. He came in every day from the sixth through the ninth, but left with empty pockets. Dominelli told Axelrod that $1 million a day was going out to investors, but that since early January, only $17 million had gone out and there was $150 million still in the pot. Unmollified and skeptical, Axelrod and his attorneys threatened they would file for involuntary (Chapter 7) bankruptcy for J. David, even though Axelrod knew that his own investors would thereupon file for Transatlantic's liquidation. According to Axelrod, attorney Robert Harlan replied he would "move Mr. Dominelli's entire operation overseas" if Transatlantic went ahead with the filing of an involuntary bankruptcy petition.

(Did Dominelli ever have any intention to buy Transatlantic, or was he only setting up the deal to get his hands on that reserve fund? Certainly, by late November Dominelli realized he was in trouble and couldn't pay anyone $2 million. "I'm beginning to believe" that the purchase offer was only a ploy to get some of Axelrod's liquid assets, says his attorney William C. Starrett II—adding, though, that he's not sure Dominelli would have been clever enough to think of it. But others in the organization might have been.)

On Black Friday (February 10) Dominelli was certain Axelrod would pull the plug with a Chapter 7 filing the following Monday. He had to get his own lick in first. He invited a large number of employees for a Sunday evening get-together at his Rancho Santa Fe estate and told them that there were administrative problems getting funds out of Switzerland, but that the company was in good shape. There had been a small run because of the bounced checks and the *Union* story, but there was still plenty of money, he claimed to his people.

Over the weekend Dominelli called a press conference for Monday morning. The recluse was emerging! In a prepared statement Dominelli said, "Let me begin by assuring investors in J. David that their funds are secure and that our firm is working to comply with requests for withdrawal of those funds. Having said that, I also want to acknowledge that J. David has problems. Although it will take time, these problems can be corrected. They are primarily the result of poor management decisions by myself."

He went on that DiNoto's suit had "no basis in fact," that J. David had no intention to file for bankruptcy, that administrative snags and "unfavorable publicity" had escalated withdrawals, and that henceforward the firm would slash its activities and employment—70 of the 270 employees would be gone by that afternoon and four offices would be sold. For the future, J. David would concentrate on foreign exchange trading, because "that is the area in which we have the most expertise and in which we have been the most successful."

To assuage unhappy investors, a "blue-ribbon team"— composed of insiders, however—would go to Switzerland and find out what was happening, but would do so "in a manner consistent with foreign bank policy" that would "maintain confidentiality of . . . interbank clients."

Dominelli admitted that the Threadneedle "trust" had not yet been set up, but he didn't say why.

"I am not going to allow rumors or innuendos to further impair a viable and dynamic company," stated Dominelli. Then he agreed to field a restricted number of queries. He averred that the Threadneedle "trust," when it was completed, would "not be related to J. David." He also said that the investor run had amounted to only 15 percent of total funds. Then he shuffled off to meetings, leaving the press to talk with investors and associates who had shown up to display support for Captain Money.

Members of the blue-ribbon panel—J. David officials Eric Johnson and Chris Kalabokes; investor William Galt, founder of The Good Earth restaurants; and Jerry Morrison, head of the local Laventhol & Horwath office—said that interbank would be audited, but that they would "maintain the confidentiality of the accounts."

I gently probed Galt, asking him if interbank required fresh funds to keep going. "The viability of the operation does not depend on new money coming into the fund," he replied. "He [Dominelli] wouldn't know how to do something like that. He is one of the hardest-working persons I have ever known in my life. I have absolute confidence in his integrity."

Charles Benton, an unhappy investor displaying a bounced check, added, "I don't think it's a Ponzi scheme. I really don't."

Several friends of J. David took up the refrain that sophisticated bankers around the world trusted Dominelli—it was just the uninformed San Diegans who didn't. Dominelli was a prophet without honor in his own city. "La Jolla is a very provincial city," commented J. David money-finder Asher Schapiro, who spends most of the year in New York but maintains a San Diego home.

But later that day Axelrod's Transatlantic, joined by a South American corporation and an individual, filed to place J. David into Chapter 7 bankruptcy, claiming they had not been paid the funds due them.

Lawyers on the case soon discovered that Dominelli and his employees had been carting off corporate records and that he was frantically trying to sell the automobiles. In short order a temporary bankruptcy trustee was appointed. The FBI said it was redoubling its efforts, and a criminal grand jury began looking into the J. David affair.

That Saturday, February 18, more than three hundred

investors held an acrimonious meeting in the gymnasium of a private school in La Jolla. Dominelli appeared and solemnly told investors he was trying to solve the problem. He was treated very coolly. The investors set up their own committee—curiously including Galt, who was on J. David's blue-ribbon team—and took steps to hire a law firm.

But efforts to organize the investors were going to be difficult. They were asked to give their names and account numbers. Many refused to do so, possibly because they were not paying taxes on their so-called profits and they wanted no attention called to themselves. "And some were concerned for their personal safety," says a lawyer.

After the meeting a horde of newspeople interviewed the shell-shocked investors. Many felt they had been had. But as is usual when a con man is being unmasked in stages, a large percentage were convinced that Dominelli had done no wrong. He was protecting the confidentiality of his investors, said some. He was protecting the lives of his daughters and of Nancy Hoover, said others. The money had been stolen from him by a gang of looters. He was just having administrative problems—hadn't he explained that clearly? He just couldn't be a crook—he was such a nice person: exceedingly kind, exceedingly humble, exceedingly generous, exceedingly solicitous.

This attitude would persist among a good number of Dominelli supporters for months, not necessarily as a manifestation of a humanitarian spirit. "Fraud victims are like rape victims, in that they blame themselves," says a lawyer. It's often simply a defense mechanism. To acknowledge that the perpetrator is a bandit is to admit that you have been duped and that there is little hope. Better to delude yourself. It takes an extraordinarily strong person to admit the truth in the early stages of a fraud's collapse.

As the meeting broke up and investors walked glumly to their cars, and reporters dashed back to their offices, people finally seemed aware that San Diego was going to be rocked by yet another financial scandal—and more people would be besmirched than ever before. "I think the really curious thing about J. David and this investment scheme is the way it cuts right through the heart of San Diego society and involves so many of the city's wealthy, prominent citizens," said Patrick Shea, a partner with Luce, Forward, Hamilton & Scripps.

Another lawyer with the same firm expressed himself in an earthier fashion: "There is more shit here than one fan can handle."

In a matter of days, the J. David scandal grew considerably hotter. *San Diego Union* gossip columnist Tom Blair asked Mayor Hedgecock if he had a J. David account—after all, he was known to be a very good friend of Hoover's. Hedgecock said he had had a "small" investment, but had removed it to remodel his mayoral home. Blair soon learned that wasn't so. The columnist went back to Hedgecock, who admitted that after the election Hoover had offered him a Rolls-Royce. Though he had turned it down, he *did* suggest she could help him with the remodeling job instead. He had borrowed $50,000 against his interbank account, and Hoover had advanced him an additional $80,000.

Then, almost daily more information about the ties of Hedgecock to Hoover and Dominelli came out in the newspapers. In his 1982 city and state financial disclosure statements, Hedgecock had failed to declare a $10,000 J. David investment. Hoover paid Hedgecock $16,000 for a trust deed, but the sale had not been recorded—and Hedgecock continued to receive the interest on it. Eventually Hedgecock amended the earlier spending report that, as a politician, he was required to submit to the state.

Quickly there was a mini-Watergate, evincing eerily familiar patterns. One paper would reveal something, and the mayor would tell a little fib. It would only motivate the journalists to dig deeper. A competing paper would look into another corner and the mayor would fudge. More digging, more dirt.

On February 24 the California Fair Political Practices Commission launched an investigation of Hedgecock. It was almost obligatory, brought on by Hedgecock's clumsy and disingenuous way of dealing with each new detail.

With a primary election looming, Hedgecock wrote 100,000 San Diego families and admitted he had made errors. He subsequently owned up to mistakes both in the handling of his finances and in his handling of revelations about them. But the display of humility came too late to head off the probes.

Former J. David insiders told investigators how employees of Thomas Shepard's political consulting firm were on the J. David payroll—and seemingly ubiquitous around headquarters. San Diego District Attorney Edwin Miller started investigating whether Hoover and Dominelli had funneled money to Hedgecock's campaign through Shepard. And the county grand jury began looking into possible criminal violations in Hoover and Dominelli's financial support of the mayor. Hedgecock charged that both Miller's and the grand jury's moves were part of a vendetta by Miller, a Democrat who had not backed him in the previous election.

In the media a juicy financial scandal had escalated into a juicy political scandal. Hedgecock, Hoover, and Dominelli, by blaming the media (primarily the *San Diego Union*) and law enforcement officials for their problems, were goading probers into digging deeper.

By this point, George Mitrovich wanted no more. Without even speaking with Captain Money or the Golden Girl, Mitrovich left them a Dear John letter, packed up his papers and political memorabilia, and departed. He moved out of the Del Mar house and said he would be devoting all his time to the City Club. Although he had brought Hedgecock and Hoover together and had been a key player in Mayor Hedgecock's first election, he would not be part of the ongoing one. The rewards of participating in local political campaigns were too few, he professed.

When asked about his involvement with J. David, Mitrovich insisted that he had been almost entirely engaged in community affairs, that he had not played any significant role in the company's business. It was a questionable statement. Mitrovich had organized and publicized events sponsored by the company. He had served as a public relations counsel—on business matters—to J. David. His presence had given the firm credibility it never would have had with a certain segment of the community. And he had helped create the mystique and the internal feeling of superiority that had kept the firm going.

According to Mitrovich, "Resigning was the most difficult thing I'd ever had to do in my life. Maybe in the end it was a huge scam. But if it was, it was pulled off with an adroitness and skill that you wouldn't believe. If there was any illegal activity going on, I never saw it."

Mitrovich seemed baffled to the end. The day before he

left, sitting reflectively in his office, he had asked a sales-man, "Do you believe Jerry could have been taken in by Mark Yarry?"

As the political scandal heightened, the financial im-broglio receded to the inside pages. But the dominoes were falling rapidly.

M. Larry Lawrence, who had loaned $1 million to Dominelli days before the bankruptcy and was now suing to get the airplane Dominelli had pledged as collateral, was suddenly no longer defending Dominelli. The bankers in the world's money centers might have told him nice things about Dominelli, but the cynical San Diegans had known what they were talking about, Lawrence allowed.

Edith Reid had to take her Reid-Smith into bankruptcy. Beginning in mid-February, her investors received letters stating, "Jerry Dominelli has assured us that the funds are intact and safe," but nonetheless, she wanted Reid-Smith funds back. Of course, she couldn't get them. On Febru-ary 22 she informed her investors she was going bankrupt because Dominelli's interbank fund was her major source of income. But, she added, she had some delicious real es-tate and oil and gas deals ready to go. Two days later, she asked that all her investors send her $250 each: "We are going to need a little financial help from each investor in order for us to perform on your behalf."

Shortly, Axelrod's investors took Transatlantic into in-voluntary bankruptcy. Axelrod had told one investor that he had $1.8 million on deposit in his Bermuda bank. He offered to pay investors a nickel on the dollar. But, noted the investor, if Axelrod only proposed to pay five cents on the dollar, he would be distributing only $850,000. That would leave about $1 million under Axelrod's control, and, to quote from the bankruptcy petition, "given the debtor's [Axelrod's] history of dissipating and misappropriating trust funds, there is a serious risk that, having freed the $1.8 million from the custody of Butterfield [the Bermuda bank], the debtor will dissipate, misappropriate or secrete the $1 million of the trust funds that will remain in its possession and control after its receipt from Butterfield." Starrett, Axelrod's lawyer, said that Axelrod's niggardly offer "was his only shot to protect what was there." Axelrod didn't fight the bankruptcy and the motion was quickly granted. Dominelli and Axelrod continued to communicate.

Mark Yarry left town. At first, as the company unraveled, Yarry had said he would testify in a court of law, and take a lie detector test if necessary, to exonerate himself. In fact, he made a point of saying that he had never seen a confirmation of a trade, and remarked, "I cannot confirm that it is not a Ponzi scheme." When his time to testify came, however, he took the Fifth Amendment all the way. Then he bundled up his family and went to the French Riviera.

As frequently happens in scams, the people at the core began splitting away from one another. Dominelli charged in a statement to the bankruptcy trustee that Bermuda's Bank of Butterfield "did not like Mark Yarry, because they had had some bad experience in which he had tried to pass himself off as myself, in trying to get funds wired out of the accounts." Dominelli also alleged that as the company was coming apart, Yarry had opened an account of "at least $350,000" in a London bank. Yarry initially said the account was in the name of J. David Banking. Dominelli told him to have the funds sent back. They never came. Dominelli pressed again. Finally, according to Dominelli, Yarry admitted that the funds were in his own name. And they never came back.

"If you look at the whole J. David problem, myself, through Nancy, on down to the people who worked in the offices, and to the clients, there is only one individual whose standard of living has improved in the period of time in the last three or four months, and that's been Mark," commented Dominelli.

From his outpost in France, Yarry denounced Dominelli as a "desperate" man and claimed he would return to the U.S. for any needed court appearances.

For Dominelli there was only one strategy: stall. Dominelli's lawyers insisted that the sovereign rights of Montserrat were being trampled upon. They pulled out a relatively unused gambit, the Sixth Amendment, for their client: He was being denied his Constitutional rights to legal protection because he didn't have a bankruptcy lawyer. They asserted that the Fifth Amendment applied to documents, as well as to accused individuals. The legal maneuvering suited Dominelli perfectly. It gave him time to think up new explanations for every new revelation, and it gave him time to dispatch an aide to Europe to snatch up records there. On the advice of his attorneys, he took the Fifth Amendment on most questions. Since there was a criminal grand jury probing into the matter, he had a right not to incriminate himself in the bankruptcy proceedings, his lawyers argued.

Dominelli, who had a history of not listening to his lawyers, made a crucial legal mistake acting on his own. On Sunday evening, February 19, interim trustee Earl Cantos and two lawyers went to Dominelli's estate to serve him with a subpoena. Dominelli invited them in, and they started talking. It was decided that Cantos's two attorneys should leave the conversation, because Dominelli was not represented by a lawyer. In private Dominelli told Cantos that his interbank fund had had $150 million under management and that the run by investors had drained off $25 million. Some $125 million remained, therefore, and the next day he would come and tell Cantos where it was.

But Dominelli never showed up to meet with Cantos. Then he broke two more dates with Cantos that week and also started telling the media he had never said he had $125 million. The bankruptcy judge ordered Dominelli to surrender property and to answer questions put to him by the trustee's attorneys. He refused to do either. Dominelli's criminal lawyer, Charles Goldberg, vehemently argued that the court was treading on his client's rights. The bankruptcy trustee just as vehemently argued that Dominelli was in contempt of court and belonged in prison. U.S. District Court Judge J. Lawrence Irving took command: Dominelli had "willfully disobeyed a court order" and was in contempt of that order.

Irving "did a superb job," comments a San Diego attorney. "After the way he handled these hearings, Dominelli's side was flailing at the air."

In a hot argument with Goldberg, Irving said that Dominelli had had "every opportunity to cooperate and he has refused. He has got to show me a good faith effort to comply with the order or he is going to sit in MCC [the Metropolitan Correction Center] until he does."

Dominelli *did* go to jail on February 25—but only for nine hours. He got his release by agreeing to write letters and telexes to the overseas banks, authorizing them to send his funds to the bankruptcy court. It was after midnight when

Dominelli emerged from the MCC, his powers of prevarication at a peak. He sat down and instructed a group of overseas banks to release $112.8 million to the trustee's account: $51 million from Swiss Bank Corp.; $37 million from Banco Solari Blum, Lugano; $24 million from Bank Haus Deak, Vienna; $460,000 from Bank of Butterfield, Bermuda; and $350,000 from Privat Kredit Bank, Lugano.

The bankruptcy trustee was elated, but also chary. Dominelli returned to his Rancho Santa Fe estate, and the trustee's attorneys sent wires and letters to the overseas banks, seeking release of funds. Later Dominelli would phone the banks with the trustee's lawyers sitting by his side. It was just a matter of waiting for the money to come in.

Thus commenced a daily ritual. The press would call the trustee to ask if the money had arrived. The trustee would say no, but wouldn't have an explanation. Dominelli would counsel patience. Everyone agreed it takes time to get money out of accounts in tax-haven banks. Were intense negotiations going on? Might the U.S. State Department be breaking new legal ground with Switzerland or Bermuda over bank secrecy? Maybe the secret accounts were not in Dominelli's name or in J. David's name, but in the name of an unidentified person representing Dominelli. Or maybe the money was in secret numbered accounts, and Dominelli had lied about those numbers.

Dominelli told friends that the trustee's lawyers were incredibly naive. Did they think that a tax-haven bank would release the funds to a bankruptcy trustee, even on the instruction of the holder of the account? His friends—who believed that Dominelli was stalling to protect their privacy—concurred. "Suppose you're a Swiss banker. Jerry Dominelli calls up and says, 'Hi, this is Jerry Dominelli. I'm sitting here with the bankruptcy trustee on my left. He wants you to release all my funds to him at his special account.' Do you think a Swiss banker would do that?" asked a Dominelli intimate.

By early March just a little over $100,000 had come in from the overseas banks, and Judge Irving was threatening to send Dominelli back to prison if no more funds arrived. Dominelli's lawyer said his client had been on the phone with the banks. "We can't go over there [to Europe]. We don't control these people. We've done our level best," argued the lawyer. Dominelli told me in an interview at the time that he would be delighted to accompany the trustee and his lawyers on a trip to Europe to recover the funds.

"Things get very sticky when you're dealing with Swiss bank officials," explained Charles Goldberg, and the trustee relented. Contempt of court hearings were postponed. Nancy Hoover offered to reveal where some of the assets were if, in return, the information would not be used by the trustee against her. The deal was refused and she took the Fifth.

Throughout this entire period, Dominelli was constantly calling friends and assuring them that the money would be forthcoming soon. He repeated the same story to the press. He seemed confident, and so did some of his associates, such as Axelrod. Few knew that Dominelli was scrambling to borrow the funds to make investors whole.

Meanwhile, Dominelli's lawyers were also jockeying to delay his appearance before the criminal grand jury. On

March 16 Dominelli narrowly missed one contempt of court citation by turning over twelve large file boxes of documents to the grand jury.

The first of the deep-pocket suits were filed. Groups of investors began suing everyone but the bankrupt Dominelli: his associates, such as Hoover and Yarry; the brokerage house Bache; the accounting firm Laventhol & Horwath; the law firms Rogers & Wells and Wiles, Circuit & Tremblay; and others, including individuals who worked for these firms.

The trustee's lawyers and accountants were under intense pressure. Their expenses had amounted to half the funds received—much higher than normal. Permanent bankruptcy trustee Louis Metzger, a retired Marine who had taken over from Cantos, contended that he was trying to hold costs down, but everyone familiar with bankruptcy procedure was cynical.

In late March J. David formally liquidated without a whimper from Dominelli, who was still busy trying to raise money from friends and assuring them—and the press— that the money was safe in overseas banks.

There was some word from Switzerland, but it didn't buoy Dominelli's spirits. Lugano officials who had been involved in Dominelli's creation of the Threadneedle "trust" revealed to the *San Diego Union* that they quickly had figured it was a sham. "It was not a real trust in the legal sense of the word. No one but Jerry Dominelli had any control over the investors' accounts," said Valeria Galli, a Lugano attorney who had set it up in October 1983. She had questioned why Mark Yarry was so deeply involved when it was supposed to be an arm's-length trust. Although she had asked for documentation of trading records, she said, she received none. She had warned J. David officials that they were not setting up a valid trust because, "everything, including trading activity and how much was in each investor's account, depended solely on Mr. Dominelli's word. The trust had no independent verification."

Privat Kredit Bank, which was to have been the bank for the trust, said that J. David had never had more than a tiny checking account at the bank and that it had been closed down as the scandal grew.

J. David's records in Lugano had been turned over by Galli to the Lugano prosecutor at the time the Threadneedle project was aborted. An investor who had been on the "fact-finding" trip to Lugano had called the bankruptcy trustee and told him about the records. The trustee was negotiating with the Swiss to get them back.

In early April a court clerk's error thwarted Dominelli's stalling strategy. The clerk accidentally released to the press a transcript of a deposition Dominelli had given to the trustee's lawyers on March 7. (Trustee Metzger unsuccessfully took legal steps to prevent the newspapers from publishing the material.) The transcript revealed that Dominelli had no idea how much money reposed in foreign banks or where it was. His grasp of details was shakier than ever. On the night in February when he left jail and listed the assets overseas, Dominelli had noted "51M" on a piece of paper designating the Swiss Bank Corp. account. But in the bankruptcy examination a month later, he didn't know whether "51M" meant 51 thousand or 51 million. "I was under pressure to put down some number that night. And the 51 is a number that has—it stuck in my head and I put that one down for that purpose. I really didn't know what the hell was in that account," said Dominelli. Perhaps the 51M *did* mean $51,000, not $51,000,000, he allowed, after prompting from lawyer Goldberg.

He further revealed that Swiss Bank Corp. had not been a very important account for J. David. Just a few months earlier he had continuously thrown around Swiss Bank Corp.'s name, telling people their accounts were traded out of there. When the truth finally came out, Dominelli didn't even have $51,000 in Swiss Bank Corp. He had $32,000.

In the deposition he went on to explain that he had never known what was in the overseas bank accounts. "I have said all along I wasn't positive about exactly what is in those accounts. . . . The hour, as I said, was late and so forth. . . . I think the attorneys there felt it was necessary to put something down," Dominelli related. He explained that throughout the existence of J. David, he would only periodically receive "a breakdown on approximate values" of what was in the overseas accounts.

He was, of course, dissembling. It was probably true that he was seldom sure of what was in the foreign bank accounts—after all, he had a grasp of very little about his business. But what was in those accounts *mattered* very little: At any given time, there was only a small amount of money in them. Most of the money investors entrusted to Dominelli never left the United States. It went primarily into First National Bank and then was spent on homes, cars, horses, favorite charities, subsidiaries of J. David, and the rest.

When investors realized that Dominelli had admitted a full month earlier he didn't know anything about the overseas money but that the trustee had still not cracked down, complaints grew. However, the delay was understandable. Metzger had just come on the scene, and delicate negotiations with the banks and governments in tax-haven countries were in progress. In mid-April Metzger and one of his attorneys, Ronald Orr, flew to Europe to make a final check on the existence of any funds in those banks.

Dominelli knew what they would find, and he decided he should fly off, too. Although the authorities had assured investors that Dominelli would not leave San Diego, he got away.

9

Fantasizing on Fantasy Island

"Nancy and Jerry were living in a fairy-tale land," says a close friend of Nancy Hoover's. Their dream was inevitably going to evanesce. Basic economics dictated it.

It happened on Montserrat—Fantasy Island.

J. David and Montserrat were ideally suited for each other. According to a 1983 U.S. Senate subcommittee report, Montserrat became a tax haven more by accident than by design. The island has "no general body of coherent bank legislation," said the report. One Montserrat official told Senate investigators, "Confidentiality [in Montserrat banking] is guaranteed by inefficiency."

While J. David was in operation, Montserrat was Fantasy Island only in the accounting sense. But in April 1984, two months after the bankruptcy, Dominelli actually took up residence on the little island, along with a small entourage—Parin Columna, secretaries Valerie Erwin and Debra Hart, and Hart's husband, Calman, a low-level computer operator at J. David.

On April 20 Dominelli was due in court in San Diego for another contempt hearing. By that time bankruptcy trustee Metzger and his attorney Orr would be back from Europe to report on the status of J. David accounts in overseas banks. Their pockets would be empty, Dominelli knew.

He thought he was ready with a last-ditch effort. In February and March, in his frantic scramble to borrow money, he had talked with two loan arrangers of dubious renown—Joseph Bonnano, Jr., son of Joseph "Joe Bananas" Bonnano, Sr., reputed former head of one of New York's five major Mafia families; and Jerome Gatto, who in the previous fifteen years had been in legal trouble over his lending activities and in fact had spent a year in jail for grand theft. At the time the conversations were taking place, Gatto and Bonnano, along with another son of Bonnano, Sr., were defending themselves in Sacramento against charges that they had conned investors through a scheme to sell posters of U.S. presidents.

After several discussions Gatto and Bonnano offered to loan Dominelli $125 million. It was strictly an altruistic gesture, they claimed. When he first learned of Dominelli's plight, Bonnano, Jr. had said, "Being Italian and who he is, and because of the money involved, they're going to fry him. [He's] going to take more heat than he's ever had before. If he needs any help, hey, we're all friends. Feel free to get ahold of us. We're all Italians. If we can't help each other, nobody else will."

Gatto and Bonnano agreed to the loan, but on two conditions. First, Dominelli had to come up with $125,000 in advance (a "loan financing fee"), and second, he had to obtain a letter of credit from Montserrat.

After making numerous phone calls to friends, Dominelli managed to raise the $125,000, which was given to Bonnano and Gatto by an old Dominelli friend and investor, Richard D. Mangiarelli. Dominelli was in awe of Mangiarelli, a colonel in the Marine Corps Reserve and a former professional football player. "The guy looks like a Marine whether he's in civilian clothes or not," Dominelli told Metzger, himself a retired Marine general. "About my height, he is a very stocky, very strong, bull-like man. He's got very short hair, obviously. He's very pro–Marine Corps, so he conducts himself sort of like a Marine all the time. He is a very rugged-looking guy."

Admirable assets, perhaps, but Bonnano and Gatto were not impressed, especially after one of Mangiarelli's own checks for $25,000 failed to clear. (Bonnano and Gatto say it bounced; Mangiarelli claims he stopped payment.)

That happened on April 12. Unaware of the snag, Dominelli left for Montserrat the next day, thinking he had put a $125 million loan package together. His plan was to pay off the investors in full and use the balance to launch a foreign currency trading and banking institution on the island. Then he would pay off the loan with his profits.

Such a fantasy! Dominelli had always lost badly in foreign currency trading, yet he seemed to believe he could make it this time. He even had Columna take electronic trading equipment to Montserrat. And in advance of his trip, he had written to John Osborne, chief minister of Montserrat, describing the glory the Dominelli presence would bring to the island: "Together, we can build an offshore banking center second to none and you can develop the island as you see fit." Just a few months earlier, Osborne, during a visit to San Diego, had told Mitrovich how much the "people of Montserrat" would love to have a Mercedes-Benz, and Dominelli and Mitrovich had been working on it.

Dominelli's departure for Montserrat a week before the April 20 showdown with the judge went unnoticed. Just before he was due to appear in court, Nancy Hoover broke the news. Entering the courtroom on crutches (she had injured her foot in a long-distance run), Hoover explained, through her tears, that Dominelli had left—perhaps never to return.

Prior to his departure, Dominelli had written emotional letters to his intimates: Hoover and her mother, children, and sister; his estranged wife; his children and his brother Victor; Yarry; Yarry's sidekick Colabella; investor Galt; his criminal lawyer Charles Goldberg; and his bankruptcy lawyer Herbert Katz.

To Hoover's mother, Dominelli waxed sentimental: "You're the person I owe the most to (at least indirectly) because there would be no Nancy Hoover without you. Please take care of yourself, and maybe one of these days I might be a son-in-law. Love, Jerry."

Tenderly, he wrote to his Golden Girl, "I feel like crying over all the regrets I have. . . . I have caused you so much grief by my lies, by my not relying on your advice; another lie to cover the first lie. And although this is no excuse, most lies I had always hoped to convert to reality. I was always optimistic about getting everything in order and . . . in its proper place."

It was a revelation: By this time many close observers had begun to wonder whether Dominelli *realized* that he was a liar, that he seldom had anything in the right place.

But there was an indication he was still fantasizing about himself: He told Hoover that without her, he would have been "just another Darth Vader."

In an open letter to "clients, friends and interested parties," Dominelli blasted the trustee for proceeding "in a manner that assumed everyone guilty of something until proven otherwise." It was time for an honorable man to come forward to do the trustee's job. That honorable man would be Dominelli himself. "I have decided to disburse the interbank client funds directly back to the accounts myself. This will result in a more economical, orderly and speedy transfer of funds back to the depositors," he wrote. There would be one exception: Anyone who had brought suit against "any of the J. David entities, principals or myself will have to go through the trustee to obtain their proceeds as these funds will be sent to the trustee account at First Interstate Bank in La Jolla, Calif."

Such a strategy was not only unprecedented, it was also illegal. So was his trip to Montserrat, for that matter, since he had been told by the judge that he could not travel outside California. (The court had even taken his passport away from him, but he didn't need it to get to Montserrat.) And he had missed the contempt hearing, after which he surely would have been jailed.

(I had egg on my face. Two weeks earlier, an investor told me he had heard that Dominelli planned to give the money back himself. I said it was so preposterous that I wouldn't even look into it. Similarly, the day we found out he had left the country, it was rumored he was in Montserrat. I said that was absurd. Even Dominelli wasn't dumb enough to go to Montserrat, where his pursuers would look first and where the British still had some authority, I stated with assurance.)

As soon as Dominelli's letters were made public, and it was revealed he *was* in Montserrat, the media descended on the tiny isle with a vengeance.

The reclusive Dominelli may not have understood the media, but he did understand the pressures of the capitalist system: He knew that if the newspapers, television stations, and radio stations had gone to the expense of putting reporters on the island, they would want to get their money's worth in exclusive news reports. He also understood that to get access to him, most reporters would refrain from writing negatively about him, even from asking him tough questions. The reporters themselves realized that Dominelli was calling San Diego every day to find out what each correspondent had said about him.

In this environment Captain Money lied like a trooper. And the reporters sent his nonsense back to the mainland with very few caveats.

Assuming his most sincere expression, Dominelli told reporters that he was going to reestablish his foreign currency investment business on the island. "Dominelli Vows To Rebuild Empire," screamed the headlines. Only a few astute observers were asking, What empire? Why bring his trading equipment when he had hardly done any trading before?

Dominelli's normal penchant for prevarication had taken a disturbing turn. He seemed to be bordering on derangement, disorientation, or at least detachment from reality. Maybe the deluded Dominelli *did* believe he would restart his business and pay off his $125 million loan from Gatto-

Bonnano with foreign currency profits. Given his dismal track record, if he really thought that, this was a case for psychiatrists, not lawyers. There was at least one investor, a physician, who had suspected two years earlier that Dominelli might be insane. He wondered if Dominelli's paralyzed eye muscle was a sign of a brain tumor.

On Montserrat Dominelli's imagination was working overtime. He vowed that once he became profitable again, he would return to La Jolla and sue the people who had brought his business down. He boasted that he already had $40 million or $50 million in pledges from people who wanted him to invest their money. Minister Osborne claimed that he, too, had heard from people who said they would invest with Dominelli through Montserrat, as long as the IRS wouldn't find out about it.

Dominelli promised to pay off the original investors by April 30 and with funds not tied up in any long-term investment. Naturally, he did not explain that he was alluding to the $125 million he still believed would be provided by Bonnano, Jr. and his partner Gatto. Many investors thought that Dominelli *was* going to return funds. Hoover claimed to believe it. "He's the kind of person who would spend the rest of his life trying to pay back his investors. . . . He's that sincere," she said.

Then Ronald Orr and Louis Metzger returned from Europe. Dominelli had sent them on "a wild goose chase," said Orr. "We have exhausted every lead Mr. Dominelli has given us. Mr. Dominelli lied to get out of jail." The judge ordered Dominelli's arrest, and government agencies, including the FBI and the State Department, began looking into the logistics of recovering a fugitive from Montserrat.

But Dominelli insisted, "I'm not a fugitive. The only thing I violated was the arbitrary way this was handled by the court." He considered his offense no more serious than missing a court appearance for a traffic ticket.

Dominelli cursed Metzger for going to Europe and said Metzger was "trying to justify his own stupidity. He should never have gotten on an airplane with Orr and flown over there." They should have taken *him* along, said Dominelli, who added, "They're idiots." But in the next breath, Dominelli claimed that Metzger really believed the money "is there" (in Europe) and said that his lawyer (Herbert Katz) was negotiating with Metzger on the matter. (Metzger vehemently denied that, and Katz, who by this time had had enough of Dominelli and was planning to resign as his bankruptcy lawyer, never confirmed it.)

Meanwhile, Montserrat leaders were having second thoughts. With reporters racing all around the island, they wondered whether the exercise was worth it. At first, it seemed to be. "The publicity is such that we could not pay for it, and it is free. People will now have heard of Montserrat as an offshore banking center. It is up to us to capitalize on the press and show we are a responsible country," remarked Parliament member David Brandt, a confidant of Osborne's who had initially set up Dominelli's "bank," but by this time, curiously, was working for the bankruptcy trustee. Osborne agreed that Dominelli's presence could be great for the people of Montserrat. (Certainly, it would be great for *two* people of Montserrat—Osborne and Brandt: Dominelli later revealed that both had presented him with a "wish list." They denied it, but Brandt allowed that some public projects might have been discussed.)

From the outset Osborne insisted publicly that Dominelli would have to tell all—how much money he had and where it was. Further, said Osborne, "I will force him in whatever way I can to return the money [to investors]." Dominelli promised to provide Osborne with an investor list and information on where all the money reposed, though he had refused to comply with similar requests by U.S. authorities. This was a different case, he explained, because Montserrat would not turn the records over to U.S. authorities. "I upheld the laws of Montserrat over a judge telling me I had to turn over a list of investors to him in the United States," he said. Montserrat's banking laws "took precedence" over U.S. laws, Dominelli claimed.

But Dominelli had not changed. He missed his first deadline to submit the records. It was an administrative problem, he explained: He and his assistants had to do everything by hand. He would have the records the following day.

The plea of hard clerical labor had a hollow ring. Dominelli and his entourage were residing in a lavish villa overlooking the ocean, and his assistants seemed to be living the good life. Dominelli spent most of his time on the phone and owed the local phone company almost $4,000.

Over the next few days, Brandt and Osborne grew more and more uneasy. Brandt was belatedly concluding that there was a credibility gap: Dominelli "said one thing one time and another thing another time." Osborne, too, had doubts, and said, "I'm not sure the guy is genuine or dishonest. I don't know."

To find out, they turned, not surprisingly, to Great Britain. And since Brandt was an agent for the bankruptcy trustee, and U.S. officials were seeking Dominelli's arrest and extradition to the U.S., they were talking with American officials, too.

Dominelli had made several critical mistakes in fleeing to Montserrat, and they all contributed to his undoing at this point. The first was to assume that Montserrat, a crown colony, wouldn't consult with the U.K., which knew Dominelli well. And he perhaps didn't realize that the final decision on whether he would remain rested with Governor David Dale, Queen Elizabeth's representative on the island.

Second, Dominelli hadn't done his economics homework. Brass-plate banking had receded as a source of Montserrat revenue in the previous year and was far overshadowed by tourism. The island was more sensitive to negative publicity than he realized. Dale, obviously influenced by the U.K., was particularly sour on the brass-platers. In recent months Montserrat's deeply inculcated Victorian morality had been asserting itself against the banking hijinks, Dale explained to the press.

Dominelli's third and most obvious error was to publicize his flight. One of the letters he wrote before he made for Montserrat was a press release for his lawyer to issue. But does a base runner planning to steal second inform the opposition's first baseman of his intentions?

Thanks to his public relations efforts, the story of Dominelli's escape was making headlines all over the world, including Montserrat. Although the government-run radio station on Montserrat kept silent about Captain Money's presence, the taxi drivers, who double as town criers, trumpeted Dominelli's every move. The island's weekly newspaper—run by Howell Bramble, brother of Austin Bramble, head of the opposition Progressive Democratic

Party—was having a field day. The Dominelli story was the opportunity the brothers had been looking for to embarrass Osborne and Brandt.

The pressing question still went unanswered. Why hadn't Dominelli come up with the documents he had promised Osborne? The Montserratians had no way of knowing then that Dominelli's loan from Gatto and Bonnano had fallen through. Dominelli had no money at all. His $4,000 worth of phone calls hadn't raised any more, and he couldn't even pay the phone bill.

The U.S., Great Britain, and Montserrat were engaging in three-way diplomacy on the issue. "We are quite concerned about this chap," said a spokesman for the British Foreign Office. Finally, Dale had had enough. On April 27, two weeks after Dominelli had arrived, he was told to leave by the next morning. Dale signed an expulsion order: Dominelli was officially an undesirable. The Royal Montserrat Police Force immediately took off for Dominelli's villa. They searched the place and found two handguns—two more reasons for throwing the book at the fellow who had upset the isle's serenity.

That was the final blow. On Dominelli's last evening in Montserrat, *Wall Street Journal* reporter Fred Muir asked him tough questions for half an hour. Muir wrote, "Mr. Dominelli was a broken man. He repeatedly drifted off in midsentence without returning to his original thought. He also kept contradicting himself. He first said that he deliberately misled the court trustee about the location of remaining investor funds, but later claimed Swiss bankers lied to the trustee when they said J. David didn't have any funds on deposit."

Dominelli was asked if he was living in a fantasy world.

Was he a pathological liar? Was he, as some San Diegans were saying, out of touch with reality? Dominelli said he couldn't comment on such questions. But he did say he had his next tax haven selected. This time, he wasn't going to let anyone know which island it was.

The next morning the Dominelli entourage, looking confused and depressed, showed up at the airport. There was no evidence they had hired a plane to take them off the island. As egrets, goats, and bleary-eyed reporters stood by, the J. David people suddenly grabbed a pilot and bargained with him. He filed a flight plan for Guadeloupe. They boarded the plane, and it took off just before 8:00 A.M. But the omniscient cabbies pointed out that the plane had changed course: It was headed for Antigua, not Guadeloupe.

Dominelli had erred again. He hadn't taken into account that Antigua is also in the British West Indies. The Montserrat expulsion order was honored by Antigua—and taken a step further. Montserrat had only expelled Dominelli, but Antigua decided to return him to the U.S. Dominelli argued with Antigua officials, claiming that his lawyers had negotiated with the U.S. government and that there was no longer an arrest warrant out for him. But he had no clout with anyone on the island, and the Antiguans put him on a plane for Miami.

Dominelli would later say with a straight face that Antigua had only been a stopping point, that he had intended to return to the U.S. Even though an armada of reporters was following him, he was certain he could get back to the U.S. secretly, confer with his lawyers, and then turn himself in for arrest, Dominelli contended.

But that scenario was never acted out. Upon landing in

Miami, a subdued Dominelli was clamped into handcuffs and charged with bankruptcy fraud, conspiracy, and contempt of court for fleeing California. The Harts, who had gone on a mysterious trip abroad prior to the Montserrat rendezvous, were also arrested. After a brief hearing in Miami, the entourage was hustled back to San Diego. Following more hearings Dominelli was returned to jail, and the judge let it be known that he would sit there until Dominelli either revealed where the money was or admitted it did not exist. His bail was set at $5 million. He was informed that a joint FBI-IRS grand jury was also looking into other areas, such as mail fraud, wire fraud, illegal money laundering, and racketeering. Three weeks later, charges against the Harts were dropped.

Before June was out, two of Dominelli's respected lawyers, Katz and Goldberg, had resigned. Both had become increasingly disgusted by Dominelli's antics, as well as by his refusal to cooperate with them. And they wondered how they would ever be paid. Shortly thereafter, Dominelli announced he had a new attorney: D. Gilbert Athay, a Salt Lake City lawyer who represented Gatto. Athay said his first job would be to get Dominelli's bail reduced.

But the U.S. Attorney's office made a surprise move: It objected to Athay on the grounds that Gatto and Bonnano had never intended to loan Dominelli $125 million. They just wanted to fleece him of the $125,000 "expense money," the U.S. charged. The government noted that Gatto had a history of taking desperate people's money as an advance on a loan, then never delivering the loan. It was just another example of an "advanced fee scheme," argued Robert Rose, Assistant U.S. Attorney.

As an attorney who had been instrumental in the transaction, Athay had a conflict of interest and could not represent Dominelli, the U.S. Attorney's office claimed. Athay testified before the grand jury for two and a half hours about the matter. The judge ruled for Athay, and he remained as a lawyer for Dominelli. The grand jury hasn't yet decided whether Gatto and Bonnano should be indicted. If it turns out that Gatto and Bonnano indeed had no intention to lend the money, then Dominelli's fateful Montserrat trip had been futile from the start. (Later, Gatto went to jail after being indicted for fraud in an unrelated matter, and Bonnano was indicted on drug and bookmaking charges.)

With Athay calling the shots, Dominelli's lawyers maneuvered to get his bail lowered and spring him from jail. But no more money was coming in from the overseas banks, and the trustee's lawyers wouldn't change their stance: "We want the money or the truth," said Orr. If Dominelli wouldn't come through, he could "stay in for a life sentence." The judge agreed.

"I always thought Dominelli would be happy in jail," remarked a former official of the firm. "There's no sun to worry about. It's dark, just the way he likes it. I always thought he liked it best when the J. David offices were in the basement below the Mexican restaurant."

Another official complained, "Everybody who was in the organization is suffering. Yarry has lost thirty pounds. I haven't got a job. Dozens of other guys don't have jobs. People are depressed and suffering physical symptoms. But Dominelli sits there in the jail happy. He is exercising and staying fit." (Indeed, he was a hero to prisoners, who stole his underwear from the laundry, cut it into fifty pieces, and distributed them as good luck charms.)

But Dominelli did *not* like jail. Finally, in a bid to get out, he confessed: He had been lying about the existence of $112.8 million—indeed, in early February he had had only $6 million. He had dissipated most of the money he had taken in from investors. He stated that $25 million to $30 million had gone to repay investors in the last few months of J. David's operations. He also had lost some money trading, he admitted. According to the attorney for the bankruptcy trustee, most of the rest had gone for the homes, the cars, the loans, the charitable gifts, the subsidies to the other operations of J. David.

In a hearing August 21 before Judge Irving, Dominelli showed no sign of contrition. The judge had to come down hard before Dominelli finally said, "I suppose you'd have to say I was lying."

Dominelli was still living in a fantasy world. Judge Irving pointed out that he had been spending investors' money, but Dominelli kept insisting it was "company money." People in the courtroom could barely refrain from laughing, and Judge Irving had to swallow hard. But maybe Dominelli really *didn't* understand whose money he was spending. All along, it seemed that even though the investors' profits were a figment of his imagination, he believed he was entitled to 20 percent of those profits.

Nevertheless, Dominelli had essentially admitted what many already knew: He had been running a Ponzi scheme at least since mid-1981, when he set up the Montserrat "bank" and started selling himself as a genius at foreign currency trading. It had been an amateurish, financially unsophisticated Ponzi scheme. "Some of these Ponzis can go on for years. If he'd just invested the money at 10 or

12 percent instead of spending it, it might be going on now," said a law enforcement official.

The lawyers pressing deep-pocket suits against J. David's service-providers rejoiced. "Dominelli's confessions make it a lot easier. I'd have had the burden of proof" in establishing that it was a Ponzi scheme, noted one.

"He [Dominelli] sent statements to investors saying they had substantial sums on deposit, and he has admitted the funds weren't on deposit. He has not only diverted the investors' funds but converted them to his own uses. If you analyze his testimony, he has admitted operating a Ponzi scheme," said Michael Aguirre, the San Diego attorney suing law and accounting firms and Dominelli's associates.

Even after the confession, Dominelli's bid for release failed. The judge lifted the contempt charge, but his bail remained at $5 million. He couldn't begin to reach it. He returned to jail.

Since, in effect, Dominelli had already confessed to some of the charges against him, the government decided to bargain with him and to try to get more information in return for a guilty plea on some of the other charges.

While the plea bargaining was going on, the grand jury indicted Dominelli on twenty more counts of bankruptcy fraud, perjury, contempt, mail fraud, wire fraud, interstate transportation of securities taken by fraud, and aiding and abetting. Among the capers cited were removing and concealing records, selling the autos, attempting to raise money to buy Commodity Monitors when in fact he was paying off investors, and defrauding M. Larry Lawrence on his $1 million loan collateralized by the airplane.

When appearing in court to plead innocent, Dominelli looked paler and more disoriented than ever. His hands seemed to shake as he pushed his glasses back up on his nose.

The worst lay ahead. Dominelli knew it. But at least for the next several months the public's focus would be not on him but on the political aspects of the J. David affair.

10

All This __and__ City Hall

In early 1983 an FBI investigator interviewed a former J. David employee—a prominent San Diego Democrat. The FBI wanted to find out whether Dominelli was running a Ponzi scheme. The former employee didn't know, but he was sure of one thing: "They're buying the mayor's job. They're corrupting the place and they're doing it in the name of good government." The FBI widened its investigation into J. David's activities, looking into the support that Hoover and Dominelli were giving Roger Hedgecock.

For an investigator or prosecutor, a case on the financing of a political campaign is usually extremely frustrating. On the one hand, the public wants untainted politicians, so there are strict laws on campaign financing. But on the other, in many states and localities it's impossible to win an election without breaking those laws. It's like college football: You can't have a winning team without violating the rigid recruiting rules. So everybody cheats—and the public looks the other way. Occasionally, a school gets caught, and then every other school, although doing the same thing, heaps scorn on the offender.

San Diego has very unrealistic campaign financing laws. A city ordinance limits contributions to $250 per person and bans businesses, partnerships, unions, or Political Action Committees (PACs) from donating. Thus, local political fund-raisers complain, the law blocks politicians' access to the very groups that are set up to dispense money. By contrast, the state of California permits unlimited political donations from corporations and other organizations; most contributions are acceptable if they're disclosed. The San Diego law is so severe that "it's almost unworkable," says a pro who has managed three major campaigns in the city. "Furthermore, people are confused. They can write a check on their business for someone running for U.S. Senate or the California legislature, but they can't do that in a San Diego city election." Obviously, if someone wants to give $1,000 to a candidate, he simply finds three other people to say they gave the other $250 increments. Often it's the donor's spouse or children. As a state investigator wryly noted, San Diego juveniles manifest amazing interest in local political elections.

The person running for a major San Diego office faces a problem: What is legal at the state or national level is illegal locally. If candidates and contributors evade the local law, they have to fudge on their state campaign filings, too, lest they be caught at the local level.

Nancy Hoover had publicly stated she wanted to be a power broker in San Diego politics. She and George Mitrovich had been close to Roger Hedgecock and Thomas Shepard, a Hedgecock ally and political consultant, since their days in Del Mar. Hedgecock, a specialist in environmental law, had been Del Mar attorney while Hoover served on the council.

Hedgecock is a bit of a political enigma. He is intelligent, articulate, charismatic, and persuasive, with an uncanny feel for public sentiment and particular support among minorities, such as blacks and gays. He has never been defeated for political office. He looks a little like Abraham Lincoln and acts the same way—rough-hewn and solicitous of the little people's concerns.

Throughout his career Hedgecock has been a maverick. Nominally a Republican, he is liberal on environmental questions, but relatively conservative on fiscal ones. This gives him a huge constituency, because San Diego's liberals and conservatives, generally speaking, are united on one point: They don't want their city to become another Los Angeles. Conservatives greatly outnumber liberals, but even many conservatives would prefer slow economic growth to seeing their city bulldozed, coated with concrete, and plastered with tacky homes.

Pete Wilson, San Diego mayor from 1971 to 1983 and now a Republican U.S. senator, was the first to pull together a left-right coalition of voters who would sacrifice economic growth to avoid clogged highways, industrial and vehicular pollution, and a rapid population increase. These voters tend to favor nonpolluting industries such as high tech and tourism, development of the inner city, growth moratoria in individual communities, and limits on industrial expansion. Since Southern California—San Diego in particular—faces major long-term water problems, the growth management position makes sense economically. It's not just a matter of improving the quality of life.

The establishment is split on the question. Retailers, the construction industry, lending institutions, and others who profit from rapid economic expansion vehemently oppose the no-growthers and slow-growthers. But some quintessentially proestablishment, wealthy movers and shakers—especially long-time San Diegans—prefer slow growth. Historically the Chamber of Commerce has had to walk a fine line between the two establishment factions.

Politicians are divided on the issue, too. As a rule, the more conservative politicians favor fast growth and the liberals want to slow it down. But the politician favoring slow growth doesn't get campaign funds from the construction industry. The progrowth businesses contribute big money to candidates who can defeat the slow-growthers.

Some slow-growthers became disenchanted with Pete Wilson, believing that once he had begun aspiring to higher office (he lost in the gubernatorial primary before winning his senate seat), he ignored his environmentalist constituency to gain financial support from the wealthy construction companies. Roger Hedgecock, although ambitious for higher office, has never cozied up politically to progrowth interests. Throughout his meteoric rise, he has been bitingly critical of the San Diego establishment, its progrowthers in particular.

While he was attorney for Del Mar, Hedgecock would often take aggressive legal positions on environmental questions. "He would say, 'We're special here. We can do that.' Hedgecock, Hoover, and Shepard considered themselves the elite. They were self-righteous. Rules didn't apply to them," recalls a powerful San Diego political organizer. It was during this period that the Del Mar coterie—led by Hoover and Hedgecock—gave themselves the smugly self-effacing monickers "The Insatiables" and "The Del Mar Crazies."

Maureen O'Connor, the prominent San Diego Democrat who had snubbed Hoover at the 1980 Democratic convention, was also running for mayor. She is married to one of the richest men in town, Robert Peterson (who, coincidentally, had been a partner of Dominelli's in the refinancing of Yuba Natural Resources). Since under San Diego law there is no limit to how much money a candidate or candidate's spouse can give to the campaign, O'Connor would be a formidable candidate.

But Hoover had money to spend, too, and she set her sights on Hedgecock, who had been a county supervisor since 1976. There was a stumbling block, however: Hedgecock was disgusted with her for divorcing George Hoover to take up with Dominelli.

In public Hedgecock's style is to be outspoken. In private he is outrageously so. He has offended numerous city officials with his highly personal, vitriolic attacks on them. One of his marks was James Hamilton, the expert on campaign-financing law in the San Diego District Attorney's office, who happened to have spent several years in the Imperial Valley desert before coming to San Diego. After he criticized Hedgecock a couple of times, Hedgecock started calling him "that sunbaked flunky." Hedgecock once denounced an opponent as "mentally ill." And he incurred the enmity of lawyers and other civil servants by continuously downgrading their skills.

In 1979 and 1980, when Nancy Hoover was divorcing George Hoover, Hedgecock aimed his invective at her as well. According to some who know him, he denounced Hoover and Dominelli in the crudest of terms.

It was Mitrovich's job to bring Hedgecock and Hoover back together. According to Alfred O'Brien, a former J. David official, he and Mitrovich had lunch with Hedgecock at the Hilton, and Mitrovich told Hedgecock he would have to stop bad-mouthing Hoover if he wanted her financial support in his mayoralty bid. Mitrovich can't recall making such a statement, but, in any case, Hedgecock and Hoover were soon fast friends again, and Mitrovich became one of his close advisers.

Knowing that O'Connor was likely to be his opponent, and that she would be well financed, Hedgecock—against his own better judgment, it is said—permitted Captain Money and the Golden Girl to become his personal angels. His early actions show he may have been suspicious of the J. David operation, but at least it didn't have the taint of the construction lobby.

In late 1981 Hedgecock's county aide Thomas Shepard set up a political consulting firm, and in the next three years Hoover and Dominelli pumped hundreds of thousands of dollars into it. The firm occupied space in J. David's headquarters, and at least one person who was working for Shepard got her W-2 form from J. David. In 1983 Hedgecock beat O'Connor in the special election to replace Wilson, who was headed for the U.S. Senate. After Hoover and Dominelli threw their lavish inaugural party for the new mayor, it was clear there was a major new force in San Diego politics: Hedgecock and Hoover. Hedgecock was so popular that he was considered a shoo-in for the regular election to be held in November 1984. In fact it was thought he would clinch reelection in the spring primary by winning over 50 percent of the vote.

But in early 1984 J. David collapsed. It wasn't long before Hedgecock's involvement with the firm became public. At first he admitted that he had inadvertently failed to report his $10,000 investment in J. David's interbank fund on public finance forms. A few days later, however, he explained that he did not report the investment because the law did not require a politician to report investments in business entities located more than two miles outside his jurisdiction. By putting money into J. David Banking, he was really investing in a Montserrat enterprise, he argued. Some people concluded that Hedgecock was just another lawyer intent on following the letter of the law, rather than the spirit of the law.

This perception was reinforced as the mayor tried to explain away other involvements, including the $130,000 he received from Hoover to remodel his home and the $16,000 trust deed he said he had sold to Hoover but continued to receive interest on. By way of a defense he would cite loan agreements and contracts that had been "memorialized" in writing only after the news had come out. Suddenly, for the first time in his political life, Hedgecock was under heavy fire—just as his reelection campaign was getting under way.

Some of the major politicians in town, such as O'Connor, decided they did not want to get into the primary race, even though Hedgecock appeared vulnerable. Richard Carlson, a former TV newscaster and savings and loan executive—and a political novice—then jumped in with considerable establishment support. Rightly or wrongly, he was perceived as the candidate of the establishment pro-growthers. Carlson had one physical liability: obesity. The slow-growthers, wanting to play up his savings and loan background and establishment backing, were quick to turn this liability to their advantage. All over San Diego posters appeared featuring Carlson's profile with a big X through it and the words No Fat Mayors. Carlson's double chin clearly had a double meaning: It stood for the progrowth establishment members who backed him.

The public soon learned that Carlson, like O'Connor before him, had a rich spouse—an heiress to a huge food fortune. And Hedgecock's supporters began asking voters: "What's the difference between a candidate that takes money from questionable people and one that is rich enough to fund the campaign himself? Do you have to be rich to be mayor of San Diego?"

Political pros suspected it was just a matter of time before there would be official charges against Hedgecock. FBI investigators already had information on the financial relationship between Hedgecock and J. David. A criminal grand jury and California's Fair Political Practices Commission (FPPC) had started investigating Hedgecock's monetary ties to Hoover and Dominelli and other aspects of his campaign financing. The district attorney did not have time before the primary to get an indictment, so he filed a civil suit charging that Hoover and Dominelli illegally funneled $357,000 into Hedgecock's 1983 campaign. The DA felt he would be criticized if he sat on this evidence until after the primary vote. Hedgecock supporters saw it another way: They charged that the DA was trying to get the mayor defeated in his reelection bid.

Hedgecock's defense strategy was three-pronged. First, he apologized to the voters for his early splayfooted handling of his finances and the revelations about them. Then, he charged the press (mainly the *San Diego Union*) with trying to smear him, and finally he accused District Attorney Ed Miller of waging a vendetta against him. Although primarily a Republican paper, the *Union* had backed O'Connor in the 1983 special election. Miller, a Democrat, had also supported O'Connor.

At first, the strategy only whetted the press's appetite. But then Hedgecock got a break. On April 20 the *Union* reported that investigators had uncovered as much as $400,000 in unexplained funds in bank accounts controlled by the mayor, and the grand jury was looking into it. Hedgecock demanded a retraction on that point and seventeen others. The *Union* retracted the statement about the bank accounts and two other statements, but stuck with the rest of the story. Unsatisfied, Hedgecock filed a $3 million libel suit. After much legal jockeying, the *Union* backed down and issued a major retraction on July 25. By giving some credibility to his charge of a smear campaign, the retraction gave Hedgecock a big boost.

Hedgecock's strategy had worked—the press backed off. As eyebrow-arching details of investigators' findings surfaced, reporters, especially from the electronic media, were reluctant to ask the mayor tough questions. Hedgecock remained center stage by contending that he was the object of a vendetta.

"Early on, there had been good, solid, aggressive reporting concerning the shakiness of the Dominelli empire. Then, there had been good, solid reporting that established the relationships between Hedgecock and Hoover and between Hedgecock and Dominelli," says Steve Casey, special assistant to the district attorney, and a former newsman. "But once Hedgecock emerged as a criminal suspect and launched his defense-by-intimidation technique, then a lot of the sharp questioning faded. . . . The press didn't make him accountable for his inconsistent statements."

Hedgecock supporters, however, still believed that the *Union* and the law enforcement authorities were out to get the mayor. As the primary neared, many people viewed the entire matter as an attempt by the establishment to put a progrowther in city hall.

Hedgecock vehemently denied that he received any of the money that J. David paid Shepard. He asked the court to throw out Miller's civil suit because, among other things, the evidence had been gathered in secret by a grand jury. And he demanded that Miller give a deposition under oath, stating his reasons—particularly political ones—for filing the suit.

Hedgecock won the spring primary against Carlson and minor candidates, but didn't achieve the 50 percent plurality required for election. There would be a runoff in November. Even though Carlson was a weak candidate, political pundits were saying Hedgecock was in deep trouble.

The view was greatly reinforced when the bombshell hit: On September 19, less than two months before the election, the grand jury indicted Hedgecock, Hoover, Dominelli, and Shepard on one count of conspiracy and fourteen counts of perjury for their roles in Hedgecock's 1983 campaign. Although some of the counts were later dropped, all the defendants remained under indictment. All pleaded not guilty.

The grand jury charged that Hoover and J. David illegally pumped $357,000 into Hedgecock's campaign through the Shepard consulting firm, that county employees were working on Hedgecock's campaign during work hours, and

196

that a number of donations had come in illegally. The indictment listed fifty-seven overt acts in furtherance of the
conspiracy, including Hoover's financial help in Hedgecock's home-remodeling project. Hedgecock was cited on
twelve perjury counts for incorrect filing of campaign contribution, income, and loan disclosure statements, as well
as on the conspiracy charge. Conviction on any of these
counts would lead, under California law, to Hedgecock's
removal from office. (Once the indictment came in, the DA
dropped his civil suit.)

Hedgecock didn't appear before the grand jury, but five
days before the indictment he submitted a lengthy letter
(not sworn testimony) explaining his position on the major counts. Miller refused to pass along the letter to the
grand jury, however, saying that exculpatory evidence had
already been presented, and Hedgecock's material was basically argumentative rhetoric, not new evidence.

That was all the ammunition Hedgecock needed for his
TV appearances on the day of the indictment. "The district attorney is the one who has embarrassed San Diego,
not me," he railed. Without even reading the indictment,
Hedgecock stated, "I am not surprised because I have
known for a week that the district attorney kept from the
grand jury evidence submitted by me that conclusively
demonstrates nothing was done wrong by me or by my
campaign committee."

Miller, a competent if colorless lawyer, denied Hedgecock's assertions, yet lacked the charisma and forceful-
ness of the media-savvy mayor. Some powerful San Diegans
such as Senator Wilson said there was no evidence that
Miller had any hostility toward Hedgecock. But the may-
or's charges seemed to stick.

The broadcasts of the TV stations favored Hedgecock. The newspapers ran lengthy stories on the indictment—including the mayor's letter to the grand jury—but the fine points were lost in the wake of Hedgecock's performance, which was magnificently orchestrated for the electronic media.

In the weeks before the election, the whole Hedgecock affair seemed to become a battle between the forest and the trees. The trees were a myriad of specific, complex charges on whether the mayor had properly reported the money he received for his campaign. The forest was the broader issue: The people seemed to be saying that the campaign laws were probably too stringent, and, in any case, Hedgecock's campaign financing was a matter that the court would decide. Meanwhile, the people were worried about their *real* trees. Hedgecock's slow-growth coalition was asserting itself: The growth management issue was so overriding that even the grand jury's charges could not smash it.

The public was oblivious as Hedgecock and his lawyer Michael Pancer (who was also Mark Yarry's lawyer) made statements that did not hold up under examination. For example, Hedgecock and Pancer complained that the grand jury had *admitted* it sped up its procedures to bring the indictment before the election. Referring to the grand jury transcripts, Pancer stated, "The District Attorney's purposeful political motivation is revealed when their [sic] deputy tells the grand jury that it is important they indict just prior to the election so as to influence the voters."

In fact, the DA's deputy had made a neutral statement to the jury: "If we haven't got this resolved by the eighth of October, I'll run into a problem. We very much want to get this resolved so that whatever happens, the electoral process can have time to react and the people can make judgments based upon merits and not upon where all of us stand procedurally."

Pancer also noted that Alfred O'Brien, the former J. David employee who had testified that he and Mitrovich had had a critical lunch with Hedgecock about Hoover, was "a political opponent of the mayor's." Pancer asserted that O'Brien's statement was "proved to be untrue" by other testimony. And what was the testimony that *disproved* O'Brien's statement? It was none other than Mitrovich's testimony.

And what did Mitrovich's testimony disprove? His words, after a fashion, speak for themselves. According to the transcripts, Mitrovich was asked by the DA's attorney, "Mr. Mitrovich, the question is, did you at any time tell Roger Hedgecock that he would have to make some form of peace or change his behavior with regard to Nancy Hoover in order to get her support in his quest for the office of mayor?"

Mitrovich replied, "I don't rule out the possibility that I encouraged him to effect whatever reconciliation, in terms of his relationship, but I cannot answer the question in terms of specifics, because I do not recall. I don't think—I mean, it is altogether possible that I would have said, 'I think your relationship with Nancy is something you need,' to the effect of a reconciliation, but I can't answer the question any more specifically than that because I do not recall. And I just barely recall the possibility that there was a luncheon at the Hilton involving Al O'Brien, Roger Hedgecock, and myself."

The DA's lawyer pressed on, reminding Mitrovich that he normally had "a marvelous recall of people and events and things." He suggested that "a conversation with a county supervisor who wants to be mayor about the need to mend fences with a major financial supporter might be something you'd recall."

Mitrovich allowed that he "might" have phoned Hedgecock for a luncheon date with O'Brien and himself, but he just didn't think financing entered into any discussion. "I am not—I know what I know. I do not know what I do not know. And I am not—again, obviously if you have discussed this with Mr. O'Brien, if Mr. O'Brien has a particular memory of that luncheon, and what the purpose of that luncheon was, maybe then in discussing it with him. But I don't have a specific recollection of those things being discussed. That isn't like me. That is not the point of my involvement in politics."

Among the documents introduced at the hearing was the letter on Dominelli's character that Hedgecock had sent to officials in Great Britain when J. David was trying to get a listing on the London International Financial Futures Exchange (LIFFE). The letter had said, "San Diego is indeed fortunate to have Mr. Dominelli and his company headquartered in our city." It was introduced into evidence because Hedgecock was insisting that he had no relationship whatsoever with J. David or with Dominelli— he knew only Hoover. Pancer noted, "A letter of recommendation written on behalf of J. David is of the type prepared on a routine basis for hundreds of businesses in San Diego, and the issuance of such a letter does not depend on their having supported the mayor." When Hedgecock was asked to produce some examples of other such letters, he said he would not, because it might compromise the people about whom he had written them.

The grand jury transcripts also revealed that on February 12, the day before the J. David bankruptcy, Hedgecock's aides met "to clean up [Hedgecock's] loan with Nancy Hoover," as one of the mayor's insiders put it. The group members drafted documents to "memorialize" a payment Hedgecock had received from Hoover—up to then never set on paper—and they raised $80,000 virtually overnight to pay it back. Hedgecock's campaign manager admitted before the grand jury that the aides cooked up a complex scheme by which the mayor could extricate himself from the money Hoover had extended to him (which they called a "loan"). The next day the operation was complete.

The transcripts also record testimony that Shepard and Hedgecock had reached an oral understanding about a computerized mailing list on January 1, 1982. The understanding was not put in writing until nine months later— on stationery that had not existed at the time the document was dated. Assistant District Attorney Richard Huffman called the contract "a pure fabrication," but Shepard said it properly memorialized the understanding.

Two of Shepard's aides testified that Shepard had instructed them to tell investigators, falsely, that they were volunteers rather than paid assistants. They also said Shepard had offered to pay for their lawyers. Shepard refused to appear before the grand jury and to comment to the press.

But all these details generally got buried as Hedgecock kept hammering successfully at the vendetta theme and repeating that his offenses were minor and "technical" in nature.

Hedgecock's final test came on October 16, when the

Fair Political Practices Commission announced its findings. It filed a record $1.2 million suit against Hedgecock, Shepard, Hoover, Dominelli, and two other associates, charging that Hoover and Dominelli funneled funds to Hedgecock during the campaign. The FPPC cited four hundred violations of campaign and financial disclosure requirements. Hedgecock was named in forty-five of fifty causes of action. If found guilty, his liability could be $974,662. It was the most comprehensive action taken by the FPPC in its ten-year history—the largest amount of money sought and the largest number of alleged violations and causes of action. The staff had spent three thousand hours on the case.

But once again, Hedgecock was prepared. He charged that the FPPC was playing politics: It could have taken administrative action and simply imposed a fine, but it opted for legal action to try to embarrass him before the election. As it happened, the chairman of the FPPC, Daniel Stanford, was a San Diego Republican who had opposed Hedgecock in his 1983 primary fight. "We all know who Dan Stanford is. Dan Stanford did not want me to be mayor," said Hedgecock. But there were five people on the FPPC board, and they had voted unanimously on the charges.

In any case, Hedgecock claimed, the violations were only a "rehash" of the grand jury charges, and he had answered some of them when he had filed fifteen amendments to his disclosure reports earlier in the year, when his involvement with J. David first became public.

Stanford, in town to give a speech about the FPPC's findings, allowed that there were some "technical" violations, but "there are major, serious violations [that] disclose a pattern which occurred [in] the campaign of attempts to evade and violate the local San Diego campaign ordinance." And he insisted that "the fact that I may not have endorsed Roger Hedgecock for mayor had absolutely nothing to do with this lawsuit."

Several weeks later Mickey Ziffren, another FPPC commissioner, said she was "appalled" that Stanford had come to San Diego to discuss details of the FPPC case prior to the election. His speech represented "the most blatant political act ever performed by a chairman of the commission," she stated.

As debate about the imbroglio raged, Hoover claimed that she had "invested" the $357,000 in Shepard's firm, a statement that brought laughs from politically knowledgeable San Diegans. For $350,000 one could buy *all* the political consulting firms in San Diego several times over. "For $25,000 the political consulting firms would throw their grandmothers in the deal," says a La Jolla civic leader. Political consulting firms usually have little in the way of assets and nothing in the way of profits.

But, on the other hand, "I guess the defense could argue that since Hoover's other investments proved she was a twit at investing, this was just another example," commented an attorney for the DA.

Hedgecock adopted a similar defense. As the scandal unfolded, he would laugh about his business ineptitude. He just didn't follow his investments closely, he said. His wife, Cindy, had to do all the detail work. But people who knew his investment proclivities claimed the exact reverse was true. "At 8 A.M., he knew his positions," says the broker who had Hedgecock's stock-and-bond account. "He called three times a day. If his stock was down a quarter of a point, he wanted to know why. It's bullshit that he was naive about investing." And he was even more meticulous about his real estate investments, according to those in the know.

Throughout the controversy Hedgecock continued to maintain that Shepard's firm was not simply a money conduit to his campaign, and that he knew Hoover, but had had no dealings with either J. David or Dominelli. If that was true, *Newsline*, the weekly publication Hoover poured $350,000 into, didn't seem to know it. On May 12, 1983, right after Hedgecock's election, *Newsline* editor Larry Remer wrote to Hoover and Dominelli, "I want to mine the political base of support that put Roger in office for NEWSLINE. . . . I want to leverage our relationship to the mayor's office into advertising from entities like the Transit Company . . . and from city lessees." Lest anyone suspect there was a conflict of interest, it would be done subtly, Remer assured them. While *Newsline* was attacking businesses on issues such as environmentalism, an "arm's length" entity—a public relations firm that Dominelli and Hoover would hire—would be hitting up the same businesses for advertising, he explained.

Which public relations firm would it be? "I think we need to hire Shepard and Associates, both because of the obvious clout they have (or appear to have) with the new mayor, and because of Tom's personal desire to help NEWSLINE grow. I've talked with Tom about this and he's amenable to it if you guys want to pay for it. . . . But, more importantly, the idea of hiring a firm with compatable [sic] people politically (not just with clout) is key. I really need someone who can be out hustling some big developers to advertise their subdivisions with NEWSLINE at the same time that we're taking on the developers on behalf of the environmentalists and have that someone not blink an eye," Remer wrote.

Remer also said he would comb the Hedgecock list for potential *Newsline* advertisers and donors. "Where appropriate, we'd also seek to have Roger put in a good word," wrote the crusading editor, who is known for attacking the conservative establishment for its ethical lapses.

An embarrassed Remer, who had to cut back his operation sharply after losing Hoover-Dominelli support when J. David collapsed, later explained that he jettisoned the strategy not long after he composed the letter. But he refused to say whether he gave it up for ethical reasons. In fact, he refused to say any more about it. Hedgecock claimed he knew of no such plans and never did favors for Remer.

As the election approached, San Diego was on edge. There was strong feeling that Hedgecock had been a very good mayor—even some of the establishment kingpins were willing to admit that. Nevertheless, two establishment powers, the head of the Chamber of Commerce and the county sheriff, demanded that Hedgecock resign. Both were widely criticized for it. Hedgecock deflected such opposition by alluding to the establishment "forces" that were trying to do him in. The mayor had help in making the point: A local radio talk-show host kept asking his listeners, "Who is out to get Roger Hedgecock?" In reflecting on Hedgecock's problem, people disinterred an old Watergate apothegm: "It's better to have a capable crook than an incapable honest man."

On November 1, Hedgecock's perjury and conspiracy trial began.

Five days later, on election day, the people spoke. Hedgecock was swept into office with 58 percent of the vote—about ten percentage points more than he had received in the primary, before the indictment and FPPC suit. He took the whole city, high- and low-income areas alike.

The vote proved that San Diegans didn't want to be bulldozed, and they didn't want their city bulldozed either. Even with Hedgecock standing trial on felony charges, the voters indicated they preferred to see the growth-management coalition run the city. As one political writer noted the day after the election, "Hedgecock's victory may mark the end of the traditional establishment mayoral candidate." Captain Money and the Golden Girl had at last won a round.

Their victory, though, would prove tenuous and unsatisfying. Like Richard Nixon in 1972, Hedgecock was buried under a mass of moving earth soon after his landslide win.

As the mayor stood trial, the court and the media focused on whether Hedgecock was guilty or innocent, while the voters—at least at first—didn't seem to care: They were mainly concerned whether he was still capable of governing. The mayor, for his part, kept hitting at his old themes: He had made only minor errors in filling out his financial disclosure forms, the DA's office was pursuing a vendetta, the newspapers were out to get him, the conservative establishment was trying to hound him out of office. The prosecutor from the DA's office, Richard Huffman, dismissed such talk as a "bag of trash."

At the outset of the trial, the betting in San Diego favored Hedgecock. But as the case progressed through December and January, the odds shifted away from acquittal and toward at the least a hung jury. There were too many things Hedgecock could not explain. San Diegans found it difficult to believe that the mayor could get a $3,000 check from Dominelli and consider it a check from his political consultant Thomas Shepard. They couldn't accept Hedgecock's explanation that when he received monthly interest checks from the $16,000 trust deed he had previously sold to Hoover, he erroneously thought it was rent from a tenant. They suspected he was trying to conceal details about the $130,000—characterized by Hedgecock as a loan—that Hoover had pumped into the remodeling of his home.

A businessman testified that in late 1981, Hedgecock, then a member of the Board of Supervisors, told him that Hoover would be financing his mayoral campaign through Shepard. It was revealed that in 1982, when the business man had a bid pending before the Board of Supervisors for a multimillion-dollar development, he had made out a check for $24,000 to Hedgecock's wife as a so-called loan to Hedgecock, who was at the time having financial difficulties. (The Hedgecocks, though, never picked up the check.) He had also driven Hedgecock to Los Angeles to consult with a bankruptcy attorney and had paid the $500 legal fee, which Hedgecock did not report on his state financial disclosure forms. Hedgecock played down these lapses as technicalities and claimed that he could never have told the businessman in 1981 that Hoover would be financing his campaign for mayor, because he had not yet decided to run for the office. Prosecutor Huffman asked Hedgecock why Shepard had in 1981 spent money to test Hedgecock's name identification against that of the police chief, then considered a mayoral candidate, if Hedgecock was not running for mayor. Had Hedgecock been aiming for the police chief's job? Hedgecock glumly replied that he hadn't been.

In early February, as the jury started to deliberate, public sentiment began to favor conviction on at least one of the thirteen counts brought against Hedgecock. Fully 75 percent of citizens polled by a local TV station said Hedgecock was guilty. Upon leaving city hall one evening, a grim Hedgecock greeted Mike Gotch, a city councilman who would be the favorite to replace the mayor if Hedgecock was forced to resign because of a conviction. "Good evening, Mayor Gotch," said Hedgecock.

One juror later summed up the trial this way: "He [Hedgecock] asked me to believe he was very unintelligent. I had to believe that he was [either] guilty or unintelligent, and I knew he was intelligent."

Evidently, ten other jurors agreed. The jury voted 11–1 to convict on all conspiracy and perjury counts. One juror held out on each charge: a supervisor of trash haulers in the city's sanitation department. After a mistrial was declared on February 13—exactly a year after the J. David bankruptcy—fellow jurors denounced the holdout for not considering the evidence, and some even accused him of sleeping through deliberations.

Hedgecock proclaimed the trial outcome a victory, but most San Diegans thought 11–1 tantamount to a guilty verdict. They wondered how a city employee had been seated on the jury in the first place. (Huffman later conceded that he had erred in the jury selection process.)

When the decision came in, another TV station took a poll. Sixty-one percent of San Diegans said Hedgecock could not be an effective mayor and 50 percent believed he should resign. But Hedgecock still had the support of black, gay, feminist, and environmentalist leaders, some of whom commented that, guilty or innocent, he was a better mayor than anyone else they could envision.

It appeared Hedgecock might be mayor for some time. Plea-bargaining sessions broke down. Hedgecock recruited Oscar Goodman, a Las Vegas attorney and real estate entrepreneur, to replace Pancer. Goodman, whose client list includes reputed organized crime figures, had earlier done legal work for Dominelli—and his firm had been J. David's landlord. Goodman said he would represent the mayor for a minimal fee. It was altruistic, Goodman explained: He owned a condominium in San Diego and believed Hedgecock was the right man for the mayor's job.

Goodman's presence caused the no-growth and pro-growth constituencies to think, at least for a moment, the same thought. They wondered jointly if Goodman would be a new power in San Diego real estate—and they marveled at the irony that Roger Hedgecock, the outspoken no-growther, had served as the catalyst in Goodman's rise. Despite overwhelming public sentiment that the mayor was guilty, some saw the odds shifting in his favor for the retrial scheduled to begin in late August of 1985. Goodman is a coy, charismatic courtroom lawyer. And, said people, the holdout juror in the earlier trial—a black—had become a hero in the black community and something of a media personality. A second trial might lead to another hung jury.

Meanwhile, the city's government remained paralyzed—and some considered that the most damaging legacy of J. David.

11

An Ill Windfall for the Professions

The sinking of the *Titanic* was like a corporate bankruptcy in every way except one: Lawyers and newspaper
reporters couldn't speed to the scene. A corporate bankruptcy is normally a windfall for lawyers and accountants—and if it's sensational enough, for the media, too.

The J. David debacle certainly had all the elements the
media could ask for: a spectacular collapse of a mystery
man and his socialite mistress; the embarrassment of local
nabobs; the startling incompetence, and perhaps corruption, of government bureaucrats; the acute discomfort of
local political figures and the possible downfall of the mayor;
a tantalizing whiff of the Mafia; Swiss banks; sports cars,
racehorses, and other chattels of the jet set; bizarre behavior; sexy secretaries; stonewalling and prevarication by
the main characters.

For the lawyers and accountants, the J. David collapse
seemed to promise great rewards as well. Word had spread
that fees for the trustee's lawyers and accountants might
run more than 50 percent of total recovered assets—well
above the normal rate. But percentages really don't count

in such a game: When money is involved, it's the absolute values that are important. The bankruptcy trustee, Louis Metzger—an honorable man—was doing his best to keep his lawyers' and accountants' fees reasonable. And as the J. David bankruptcy wound down, it became clear that little money would be forthcoming from the central characters. Any money would have to be recovered from the deep-pocket service providers, three of which were, ironically, law and accounting firms. Thus, it appeared that some lawyers and accountants would reap a moderate windfall, but others stood to lose big.

From an accounting perspective, J. David was a disgrace. Accountants hadn't been permitted access to the heart of the company—the covert interbank pool—thus they never knew where the money was coming from. To the profession's credit, it was an accountant who first went to the FBI. On the other hand, one of the nation's largest accounting firms, Laventhol & Horwath, has been sued for its auditing role in J. David. To be sure, Laventhol never did work for interbank. Its main mistake was to rely on the judgment of Dominelli's lawyer when it determined that, under Montserrat law, it could not audit a commodities pool. Laventhol should have noted this scope limitation in its report, but didn't, perhaps because agencies such as the SEC do not accept scope limitations.

At the outset lawyers were conspicuously angling for the official appointment as the trustee's lawyers, usually the choicest plum in a bankruptcy case. "As I looked around the courtroom, I saw dozens of lawyers. The mating dances of these big firms!" says Jeffrey Isaacs of San Diego's Procopio, Cory, Hargreaves & Savitch. The job went to Los Angeles's Gibson, Dunn & Crutcher, but it was likely there would be more than enough work to go around. In March 1984, when Dominelli officially entered Chapter 7 bankruptcy, Federal District Judge J. Lawrence Irving, who was handling the case, told a gaggle of lawyers in the courtroom that the case would become "a full-employment act for the attorneys in this geographic area. We have seen the tip of the iceberg on litigation. Floodgates will open." The floodgates opened, but not as wide as expected.

Throughout J. David's life, Dominelli had only a handful of competent lawyers. One was ex-SEC attorney Carl Duncan of Chicago's Abramson & Fox, who dropped out before the bankruptcy because he couldn't get adequate information from Dominelli. The second, Nicholas Coscia, another ex-SEC attorney, quickly figured out the scam, warned other lawyers involved, and got out, graciously staying around long enough to be replaced. The two others, Charles Goldberg and Herbert Katz, were hired after the bankruptcy commenced, but also departed because they weren't getting cooperation from their client and didn't know where their fees would come from.

It was Coscia who blew the whistle on the two lawyers who were running J. David's legal affairs, Mike Clark of Wiles, Circuit & Tremblay and Norman Nouskajian of Rogers & Wells. Though the two firms jettisoned Dominelli after receiving Coscia's letter, both would face mammoth problems, and they knew it. It was inevitable they would be sued by disgruntled investors, and Clark and Nouskajian, and their firms, would be the major targets.

Before coming to San Diego, Clark had worked as an accountant for a Las Vegas gambling casino. Initially with Wiles, Circuit, he had mainly practiced divorce law. Indeed, a physician whose wife was represented by Clark in their divorce suit was directed to J. David's interbank by one of Clark's paralegals. The doctor had come to the office to cosign his wife's tax refund check, and Clark's assistant told him of the wonders of J. David. Clark personally wooed another doctor into interbank, although he denies receiving a finder's fee for such services.

Wiles, Circuit partners who worked on the J. David account had money in interbank and made large removals just prior to the collapse. They refuse to comment on any aspects of the adventure, other than to say that the press has blown it out of proportion. The firm probably grossed more than $500,000 annually in legal fees from J. David.

Early in his career, Norman Nouskajian had primarily been a real estate lawyer. He was not considered a heavyweight in legal circles. But he rose quickly in Rogers & Wells, partly because he was bringing in so much money (probably more than $500,000 annually in legal fees) for the firm from J. David.

In early 1983, Nouskajian—with acquiescence from higher levels of Rogers & Wells—led the legal team which persuaded the California Department of Corporations that J. David's interbank contracts did not have to be registered as securities, even though notes of the law firm's meetings and internal correspondence showed that Rogers & Wells lawyers believed they did. The next year, when J. David went under, Rogers & Wells initially said that its lawyers had never worked on interbank. Later, as it became clear that Nouskajian had worked on interbank right up to its demise and that the firm had enabled J. David to persuade the Department of Corporations it did not have jurisdiction over interbank, Rogers & Wells stopped making the claim.

"Many local lawyers thought Norm [Nouskajian] was a bomb in Rogers & Wells's pants. We didn't know he was nuclear," comments a San Diego attorney.

Initially, San Diego lawyers were afraid to charge Rogers & Wells with any violations. Not only do its partners have important Republican connections at the highest national level, such as William P. Rogers and CIA director William Casey, but suing a large national law firm can be a ticket to perdition: "They have money. They have size. They can just nickel and dime you to death with documents, subpoenas, and more documents and subpoenas," says a San Diego lawyer.

Nonetheless, San Diego attorney Michael Aguirre sued Clark and Nouskajian, and their firms, for conspiring to sell securities without qualification, exemption, or registration; securities fraud; and attorney malpractice. San Mateo lawyer Joseph W. Cotchett sued the same parties on the same charges.

Aguirre and Cotchett sued Laventhol & Horwath for accountant malpractice and conspiracy to sell securities without qualification, registration, and exemption. Also charged with complicity in the unlawful conduct are Ron Massa, the insurance broker who sold the fidelity bond on Dominelli, and his firm, Rollins, Burdick & Hunter; Hoover; Yarry; and several others.

The accountant and attorney defendants unsuccessfully sought to have the actions dismissed, although their objections to a few counts were upheld. The judge hearing the cases withdrew from further participation after it was revealed that she was in a real estate deal with a partner at the San Diego office of Rogers & Wells and a partner of the firm representing Nouskajian.

Just before the filing deadline of February 14, 1985 (a year and a day after the bankruptcy), a number of other lawyers joined Aguirre and Cotchett in bringing deep-pocket suits. Now there are investor claims for more than $120 million. Ironies abound. For example, Arthur Axelrod and Theron Nelsen, aggressive merchandisers of interbank, are plaintiffs in some civil suits, defendants in others.

Rogers & Wells is generally considered to be the primary target. It has a good reputation to protect, and the attorneys representing the investors assume it has a huge insurance policy.

The deep-pocket suits are all-important, because investors don't expect the bankruptcy court to recover much. By spring of 1985, the trustee had gotten back $11 million, of which $2.5 million went for expenses (including $1 million in lawyers' fees). Costs were extremely high, in good measure because of Dominelli's chaotic bookkeeping and the necessity to negotiate with foreign countries.

Investors were fuming. "The thing that really bugs me is not the loss of the money, or Dominelli, but how the attorneys and accountants have managed to funnel almost everything they recover into their own pockets," says Simon Casady, a San Diego investor and a former candidate for mayor.

Once it was determined that Dominelli had no money, the bankruptcy trustee's major battleground became preference payments. Under the law, investors who get money out of a failing company ninety days before a bankruptcy must pay it back. This is designed to make the eventual redistribution of assets more equitable. The trustee sued a large group of preference recipients for more than $20 million, but money only trickled in. Most were planning to

215

fight it in court on the grounds that the trustee's lawyers had made errors when filing the bankruptcy papers.

In early October 1984 the trustee attempted to strike a deal with those who received preference payments: If they would ante up without a fight, they would have to return only part of what they took out. Still they resisted. It promises to be a long court fight.

Meanwhile, the trustee did the best he could to come up with assets that could be sold—the homes, cars, horses, stocks and bonds, the stake in Yuba, and so on. Nancy Hoover conceded that a significant amount of her assets came directly or indirectly from J. David, and she agreed to retain only 20 percent of the net proceeds of sales of contested assets up to $387,750. The bankruptcy estate would get the other 80 percent, and 100 percent of everything above $387,750. The investors' committee was livid about the terms given Hoover, even though she would wind up with assets of a good deal less than $100,000. All told, the trustee is expected to bring in only $30 million to $35 million.

All through his court battles Dominelli had lawyer problems. His legal strategy, plotted by his attorneys, was that he could discuss certain aspects of his case with the bankruptcy trustee, but he would take the Fifth Amendment on the major question—what happened to the money—lest he incriminate himself before the criminal grand jury.

After he lost a string of lawyers, Dominelli decided he wanted the government to provide him with legal assistance as an indigent. But to get free legal help, a person has to *prove* he is indigent. If Dominelli had done that, he would have been admitting what almost everyone by that time suspected—that the money was gone. So Dominelli, with the help of his soon-to-depart lawyer Charles Goldberg, worked up a two-tier strategy: Dominelli would claim indigence, but refuse to state under his Fifth Amendment rights whether he had any money. He refused to fill out the financial disclosure form essential for establishing indigence.

It was a legal first, said local judges. They could find no precedent for such a plea. Goldberg eloquently argued that Dominelli must be afforded the fundamental constitutional rights to both legal representation and protection against self-incrimination.

But Dominelli was not to have it both ways. Taxpayers read about his singularly brazen attempt and protested. After all, he had just come back from Montserrat, where he had lived in the lap of luxury.

"Judges aren't supposed to read the election returns, but no judge in the world is going to grant this one," said a local lawyer, and almost everyone agreed. U.S. Magistrate Roger Curtis McKee turned Dominelli down, noting, "The burden of establishing the right to appoint counsel is on the defendant. Without completion of the affidavit, the defendant fails to establish indigence." (Early in 1985 Dominelli finally did admit indigence and got a government-paid lawyer.)

In the summer of 1984 Dominelli—like Ponzi before him—became his own lawyer in the bankruptcy action. Judge Irving granted him permission, but warned him that he would be facing well-schooled attorneys. Dominelli, who had taken some law courses at night, made it through his hearings satisfactorily, but then seemed to lose interest in the complex case.

Soon, D. Gilbert Athay, Jerome Gatto's lawyer, was representing Dominelli on the criminal side. He was assisted by Nicholas De Pento, a San Diego lawyer. De Pento had served as attorney for the widow of Frank Bompensiero, a reputed San Diego Mafia chief who was mowed down in a gangland-style slaying. He had also represented Chris Petti, an associate of Bompensiero. (In a one-act play presented by the San Diego County Bar Association a decade earlier, a character by the name of "De Pimpo" solicited business beneath blinking neon lights. An indignant De Pento filed suit against the bar association, but the papers were never served.)

Coming to Dominelli's defense was an altruistic act, De Pento declared. "I'm doing this because I think an injustice has taken place in terms of the lack of representation and the turmoil in his representation." He hadn't even discussed a fee with his client, he said.

In trying to spring Dominelli, De Pento waxed more poetic than his predecessors. The opposition's declaration "lacks every essential averment in order to render No Exeat jurisdictionally permissible," read his brief. "With these principles in mind, debtor urges that the subject contempt finding should be vacated because it constitutes summary adjudication of a 'constructive contempt,' one not occurring in the direct presence of the court. Such summary adjudication, without affording the alleged contemnor an opportunity to defend, was an act in excess of, and beyond the jurisdiction of the court." The judge wasn't moved. Neither was Dominelli. He remained in jail.

Seldom do bankruptcy trials produce such theater. The court was often filled to capacity, and people had to stand outside. Even the banter among the competing lawyers and the judges led to some memorable moments. At one point a lawyer for Dominelli filed a brief claiming Dominelli couldn't release the coveted investor list because that would violate Swiss laws. Judge Irving sighed, "Counselor, haven't we been through all this before? Weren't we warned the Montserrat navy was going to be sent over here to pick up Mr. Dominelli if he gave account information?"

Trustee lawyer Ronald Orr followed up, "I guess now we have to worry about the Swiss navy."

Early on in the case, when Dominelli's lawyer Robert Harlan argued that any attempt to get Dominelli's investor list would violate the sovereignty of Montserrat, one lawyer commented, out of court, "Are we going to have to attack Montserrat to get the money? So soon after Grenada?"

Dominelli's lawyers tended to blame the press for their client's problems. De Pento, for one, lashed out at the "often inflammatory media coverage." It's true that the Dominelli caper received inordinately heavy coverage considering the amount of money involved, but that wasn't the press's fault: This was a story with a hungry market.

At the outset the self-appointed San Diego media critic, George Mitrovich, was extremely denunciatory of press coverage. He would call editors he knew and scream about stories that denigrated his favorite people, including George Mitrovich. As the truth came out, however, even Mitrovich cooled off. But by that time he couldn't pontificate about it in print: He was no longer writing a column for *Newsline*. He was focussing his efforts on opening a City Club in Denver.

San Diego's liberals had lost their most voluble spokesman, George Mitrovich—a net gain for the liberals and another loss for the conservative establishment.

219

12

Southern Californians Caught in the Tangled Web

"Now will I show myself to have more of the serpent than the dove; that is, more knave than fool," wrote Christopher Marlowe three hundred years ago.

When many scams collapse, observers ask whether the key players were knaves or fools. Was audacity part of their plan? Or were they just stupid? Was the chaos a deliberate smoke screen, or didn't they know any better? Were they cool under fire because they had deluded *themselves*? And what about the investors? Were they victims of their own cupidity? Or stupidity?

In the J. David aftermath the knave–fool question became the dominant one. In spring of 1985, an accountant for the bankruptcy trustee explained in court that nobody at J. David knew how much money was in company bank accounts. Judge Irving asked if this was a matter of "design or incompetence." Sighed the accountant, "a little of both."

In retrospect, J. David "Jerry" Dominelli's lies were star-tlingly brazen, his behavior startlingly bizarre, and his business acumen startlingly nonexistent. It's astounding that the tangled web he weaved hadn't ensnared and strangled him earlier. As journalists and investigators pieced the story together, partly from Dominelli's own confession that the money he took in was gone, it was evident that Dominelli had run a rather crude Ponzi scheme—nearly as crude as the scheme Ponzi himself had run. Almost as quickly as investors' money had come in, Dominelli had dissipated it on J. David subsidiaries, dubious loans and investments, gifts to charities, race cars and sports cars and racehorses and huge estates and ski condominiums and jewelry and art objects and memorabilia. In December 1983 insiders and their friends had smelled trouble and started pulling their money out. As word got around, the inside run became an avalanche. By the time the company col-lapsed there was virtually nothing left. Some investors continue to believe that insiders have stashed a portion of the money in tax-haven banks, but few think Dominelli or Hoover has done so. They were broke. The spree was spent.

The legal tally? Dominelli pleaded guilty on March 21, 1985, to two counts of mail fraud that stripped investors of $80 million, one count of bankruptcy fraud, and one count of evading $10.7 million in taxes. He admitted that he had fabricated his track record and investors' monthly profits, that he had lost money on what trading he did, that he had falsified corporate records, that he had diverted customers' money to his own uses, and that he had lied to the Department of Corporations to avoid regulation. "Only by soliciting and using new funds from new investors could

I satisfy demands for withdrawals," confessed Dominelli. In short, he finally owned up, it *had* been a Ponzi scheme. He could be sentenced to up to 20 years.

That hardly set the matter to rest. Investors and J. David insiders are under intensive examination by the IRS, which has reconstructed investor lists from what records are available. Hoover, Dominelli, Mayor Hedgecock, and Hedgecock's aide Thomas Shepard have been indicted on one count of conspiracy and several counts of perjury for allegedly funneling $357,000 into Hedgecock's 1983 election campaign. The California Fair Political Practices Commission (FPPC) has sued the same four, plus two others, on similar grounds for $1.2 million. And numerous civil suits remain.

One of the defendants in these cases is now on the sidelines—Dominelli himself. In October 1984, just a few days before his second round of indictments for bankruptcy fraud, and just before his political perjury and conspiracy indictments were handed down, Dominelli was talking with Hoover on a jail phone. Suddenly, he became silent. Alarmed, Hoover called the prison. Guards rushed him to the jail physician, and then to a hospital. He had suffered a severe stroke.

It wasn't surprising. Dominelli's health had been deteriorating: He had been treated for an ulcer while his company was foundering and had suffered from hypertension in jail. He had looked increasingly ashen and weak in his court appearances.

When news of his stroke got out, people wondered if Dominelli was concocting another hoax. A stroke can be faked by a skilled con artist, and Dominelli was certainly that. But a team of court-appointed physicians attested that it was the real thing. "God seems to have stepped in. Jerry Dominelli can't tell any more lies," says Sandra Kritzik.

Psychiatrists examining Dominelli found that his vocabulary had been reduced to *yes, no, yeah, I, that, Oh God,* and *all right*. He communicated by grunts and written messages, but his scribblings were difficult to comprehend. The doctors said, though, he was not insane.

But they were confused by his behavior. Dominelli had long refused to wear a hearing aid. (A judge ordered him to use one in court, however.) In the rehabilitation sessions, doctors couldn't tell if his poor responses to questions resulted from his inability to hear or from his mind's inability to process the instructions.

During one therapy session, the beeper in Dominelli's watch went off, and he scrawled on his notepad, "Telephone." The doctor permitted him to make a call. He was able to punch out the long-distance number and punch in his credit-card number, and somehow communicate by only grunting a few sounds. Those who know Dominelli were smiling. Someone with a nine-word vocabulary and poor physical coordination was able to punch out accurately more than twenty digits on a telephone and get his message across when it was to his advantage? The con artist was still at work, even after the stroke, they said.

Despite his incapacitated state, Dominelli was declared competent to stand trial. When he confessed on March 21, he could not pronounce the word "guilty." Judge Irving had to lead him through the exercise.

Now, with Dominelli's fraud case finished, prosecutors said they would continue trying to learn who *helped* Dominelli in the fraud.

Throughout Southern California, people wondered about

Nancy Hoover. After all, she had spent twenty-four hours a day with Dominelli. What was her role? Why had she only been indicted for her involvement in the election, not in the scam?

At least publicly it seemed she had decided to sleep the whole thing off. When J. David went under, she would sleep from sunup to sundown. On one of the rare occasions when she made a public appearance, she enraged investors by wearing a T-shirt emblazoned Nobody's Perfect.

In late May she came out of her cocoon to be interviewed by Tom Blair, *San Diego Union* gossip columnist. She was the Hoover of old, laughing and quipping, leaping from topic to topic. But her humor was tinged with an uncharacteristic sarcasm and flippancy. For example, noting that some of the checks that had gone to Shepard had come from a firm named Cheyney Associates, Blair asked her who Cheyney was. With her former ebullience, but not without irony, Hoover admitted that Cheyney was her fourteen-year-old German shepherd, "a magnificent, wonderful animal. I got tired of reading about these things, so I started using phony names so people wouldn't know it was me." The dog, Hoover added, "felt he made a bad deal."

The grand jury that indicted Mayor Hedgecock apparently thought so, too. Among the overt acts it cited against Hoover was the fact that no Fictitious Business Name Statement had ever been filed for Cheyney Associates.

At the end of Blair's interview, Hoover breezily pointed out that the press had made a mistake in its coverage of the gift she had offered Hedgecock. The papers had said it was a Rolls-Royce. "It was a red Ferrari," she laughed.

The interview infuriated those who had lost money in J.

David. "I had defended her. I had never called her a cold, calculating bitch. But . . . ," says Sandra Kritzik bitterly. "She's laughing at the rest of us. She's still around, smiling." Quickly, many of Hoover's former supporters started dropping away.

In the early days of the J. David collapse, Hoover had taken the Fifth Amendment. But eventually she cooperated with the investigators and the bankruptcy trustee. She tried to get immunity in return for testimony, but was refused, insist prosecutors.

There are two general theories on Hoover. One is the Rebecca-of-Sunnybrook-Farm theory, that she was hopelessly naive and didn't know what Dominelli was doing. As the scandal unfolded, Hoover had told Sandra Kritzik, "I feel as though I'm on a ship and very big waves are coming, but the captain won't tell me anything." (Handyman Parin Columna, who was indicted along with Dominelli, adopted a similar defense, what Assistant U.S. Attorney Robert Rose calls "the Nuremburg defense"—the accused admits the crime, but says he was doing it under orders from his boss. Eventually he pleaded guilty to a misdemeanor charge and got only probation.)

The second theory is that Hoover was cunning and avaricious, that she might have held Dominelli captive while she and others (such as Yarry) ran the show. There is little doubt she was consumed by greed and is a pro at Machiavellian maneuvers. And she certainly pulled massive funds out of the company—a few say as much as $6 million. Some Hoover defenders say she was mainly involved in noninterbank matters, particularly J. David Securities. However, she *did* pay the interbank money-finders and keep some interbank records, she *was* on the board of J. David Banking, and she *did* help plot the escape from Great Britain to Lugano.

Since she had had experience in the investment business, some find it incredible that she didn't realize Dominelli was doing very little trading. She should have known he was not getting confirmations; after all, she opened all the firm's mail, contend these critics. They also say that she should have known that he couldn't possibly have been earning money at the rate the two of them were spending it. Several knowledgeable persons claim she was with Dominelli when the "earnings" for investors were invented each month. "I would love to have been a fly on the wall, overhearing those conversations when they came up with the month's winnings," says attorney Kenneth Poovey. But Dominelli and Yarry both insist Hoover was not present at such times, and one prosecutor says there is no evidence she was.

In the end, Hoover's actual role may fall somewhere between the "Rebecca" and "guiltier than Dominelli" extremes. There is still plenty of spadework to be done, say investigators. Awaiting court appearances, she no longer lives on the Rancho Santa Fe estate. Her ex-husband is paying for the education of their daughter, and her children, now in their early twenties, are helping pay for her lawyers. After always siding with Dominelli initially, she is now telling intimates that his dishonesty has made her disenchanted. (But the disenchantment is not mutual; according to one investigator, "Dominelli will never rat on her.")

Still a mystery, too, is Mark Yarry's role. Many, such as former portfolio manager Robert Mengar, think Yarry engineered the foreign-exchange strategy. "I was always told that Yarry came to Jerry [in mid-1981], set him up with the offshore bank, set up the accounts, and told him he'd teach him about interbank," says Mengar. "As far as I knew, Yarry had set up the whole thing." It was Yarry who moved the money around tax-haven banks. "Dominelli didn't know anything about offshore banks, or other banks."

Dominelli feels Yarry walked off with some money, and many investors suspect it, too. Yarry left for France shortly after the bankruptcy, later went to South Africa, then returned to France. The U.S. government has not called him back, and nobody has explained why it let him go. He is a defendant in the third-party suits, but some doubt he would return to be tried. Yarry, like Hoover, is still under investigation by the U.S. Attorney. Yarry's lawyer says his client will be taking the Fifth Amendment indefinitely.

Many questions remain. Investigators looked into Dominelli's activities under the Racketeer Influenced Corrupt Organizations (RICO) statutes, a key part of the 1970 Organized Crime Control Act passed by Congress. The FBI probed whether Dominelli laundered money for hoodlums—sending cash to a tax-haven bank and repatriating it as "clean" money for a fee. He may not have had the sophistication for that, but others in the organization may have. And because he always carried great wads of cash and had a huge safe at corporate headquarters, it's possible that he accepted cash from investors who were desperately trying to get rid of it. Private investigators are looking into some apparently questionable uses of the limousine service, some unusual flight patterns of corporate jets, and mysterious money transfers, among other things.

Certainly, Dominelli had relationships with persons who

have been identified as having organized crime contacts: Gatto, Bonnano, and Glick. Las Vegas attorney Oscar Goodman, who filed incorporation papers for a Las Vegas subsidiary in 1983 and also served as J. David's landlord, has had clients such as Anthony "Tony the Ant" Spilotro, considered by authorities to be a Las Vegas front for mobsters.

Another major issue is whether the list of people who received preference payments is complete. Some investors suspect that many others—mobsters, perhaps, and Dominelli family members—got their money back surreptitiously. There is a theory that J. David always had two client lists: the respectable citizens; and the mobsters, who remained secret and were paid off before there were outward signs of trouble.

Nagging questions also remain about the role of the regulators. The California Department of Corporations and the Banking Department in particular must be made to explain their pathetically inept actions, which some believe raise the possibility of corruption. Dominelli's pools were clearly securities and should have been registered. And how the Banking Department could conclude, with the massive body of evidence at its disposal, that J. David Banking was doing no business in California defies rational analysis.

The federal regulators could have cracked down early. One former J. David employee told the FBI in 1983 that the firm could be forced to open all its books through use of a legitimate, if aggressive, ploy. The J. David Trading subsidiary was fully registered with the Commodity Futures Trading Commission. Dominelli and Hoover were listed as principals. According to CFTC rules, Dominelli and

Hoover "were subject to inspection at any time," says the former employee. "And not just J. David Trading. The FBI or Justice Department under this mandate could have gone in and demanded to see details of all businesses, whether registered or not." The FBI didn't buy the argument. The Bank of England appears to have used a similar tactic, and turned out to be the hero.

There are questions about the government's current role as well. Robert Rose, the Assistant U.S. Attorney probing the J. David scheme, has a small staff; not surprisingly, the case is moving slowly. "If only to allay public anxiety, they should have a decent-sized staff," remarks a San Diego criminal lawyer. But some suspect the government is dragging its heels because it does not want to get any deeper into the case. Hoover and Dominelli had connections with many big-time politicians. According to rumor, there are big names that have not yet come out. That's why, say some, the government has not released the names of investors obtained from Dominelli in Miami and recovered from Lugano. Some feel that in the spring of 1984, when the bankruptcy trustee was supposed to be negotiating with Switzerland over the return of the Lugano records, he was in fact negotiating with the U.S. government, which, say these cynics, was trying to protect some important politicians.

Could the scheme have been detected from inside? Former employees agree that J. David was highly centralized: All decision making was in the "throne room," as Dominelli's office was contemptuously called. Hoover and Dominelli were shrewd in shifting employees around, playing them off against each other, and making sure no two people became intimate enough to start comparing

notes. If all the employees—and investors who were constantly around headquarters—could have huddled together and shared what they knew, the whole thing might
have been thwarted, comments a former financial official
of the firm. But Mr. Inside and Ms. Outside made sure that
didn't happen.

Those on the J. David payroll certainly should have been
more alert. Numerous interviews reveal that employees
believed that people in the J. David inner circle were al-
cohol and substance abusers.

Could the service professionals—law, brokerage, and
accounting firms and banks—have prevented the swin-
dle? The courts will decide that in the third-party suits. The
suits maintain that if Rogers & Wells had not helped provide false information to the state of California, the interbank contracts would have been regulated, and the scheme
would never have gone on.

Without a doubt First National Bank knew that J. David
was commingling investors' funds with its own corporate
funds. Indeed, in setting up a loan to J. David, First National requested a letter from Dominelli authorizing the
removal of money from any account to pay for obligations
in another account that might be overdrawn. On January
12, 1984, Dominelli wrote to First National and empowered it to tap the J. David Banking account—supposed to
contain only the investors' funds—for a $248,000 check to
Hoover Farms, the Hoover-Dominelli horse stables. The J.
David Banking account, said Dominelli, should also be
charged to pay off Fitzpatrick Racing and a lawyer from
Wiles, Circuit & Tremblay. The note was an obvious example of commingling.

However, in today's "zero balance" banking, such intermingling of accounts at a bank is permissible if, from an accounting standpoint, the customers' money is kept seg-regated—that is, if any money taken from one account and transferred to another is quickly replaced. Thomas LaHay of First National says that if the books are straight, the money going out of an account doesn't have to be the same money going into it. But, concedes LaHay, that's a mighty big "if." In the case of J. David, the money was clearly not replaced. The J. David Banking account had run down to close to zero. So had the other accounts. The bank also said it was not its job to monitor accounts for irregularities such as commingling.

"The one organization that knew what was going on and could have told the others—the employees, the brokerage houses, the accounting firm, and the law firms—was First National Bank," states a former top financial official of J. David. First National strongly asserts it has no liability, and that it didn't know of the fraud until the end. President E. G. Cunningham also points out that it was First National which first closed down Dominelli's checking ac-counts.

There are known instances of checks made out to J. David Banking that were endorsed to another account at First National. The bank honored the endorsement. "If you're looking at this as a morality play, here is a question investors would ask: 'If I write a check to a particular ac-count, shouldn't it be deposited there?' " says Assistant U.S. Attorney Rose. On the other hand, comments Cun-ningham, "It's the responsibility of the bank to see who is signing the check," not where the money comes from or goes.

And there is another angle. Some feel that Dominelli had

deluded himself into thinking that in spending his investors' money, he was actually just borrowing from his
Montserrat "bank." In many Ponzi schemes, the perpetra-
tors believe they are only "borrowing" the investors' money
and will replace it later. Dominelli *did* borrow from the
Montserrat bank; a Laventhol & Horwath letter proves it.
Robert Mengar, for one, believed early in the game that
Dominelli was able to spend extravagantly because he was
borrowing from the "bank." But the "bank" had only his
customers' funds.

Should investors have sniffed out the scheme? The
Oklahoma investor did. But investors who exercised *normal* due diligence didn't figure it out. Clearly, a Monday
morning quarterback can say that no one should invest in
a scheme in which there is no paper trail, no information
on how your money has been invested, and no audit. A 40
to 50 percent annual return, with only one down month
in three years, is absurd on its face, particularly since in
the commodities business, about nine out of ten outside
investors normally lose money. Yarry even said that in his
book.

However, it must be kept in mind that to many customers, interbank was not an investment. It was purely a
speculation and a gamy one at that. And people gamble
for the same reason they climb mountains, shoot rapids,
drive cars at 110 miles an hour, or parachute for sport. Part
of the thrill is the risk.

"At first, I thought the investors were generally stupid.
But later I came to the conclusion that it was more a case
of the Greater Fool Theory. People were in it with the idea
of getting out quickly and leaving the losses to the next
sucker," says a former high official of J. David.

There's no doubt that some sophisticated investors knew, or at least suspected, that J. David was a scam. But the excitement was to get in and get out with fat profits before the music stopped. The tragedy is that as in all such scams, a high roller's less affluent employee or neighbor sees him making money in the game, and then mortgages his home to get in as an investment. When it comes apart, the investor loses everything—the speculator just goes on to another thrill.

The J. David investors fell into two basic categories. There were the "hot money," well-heeled speculators, concentrated in Palm Springs and Orange County, who were in it partly for sheer exhilaration. Then there were the "family" folks—Hoover and Dominelli's families, friends, employees. Many of them could not afford to lose their money and had no business being in the game.

It's important to remember that the rich *should* put 10 to 15 percent of their portfolios in risky ventures offering big payoffs. If they win, fine. If they lose, they take a tax write-off. For this reason, people of modest means shouldn't pursue the same strategies. Don't *invest* in a scheme in which others are *speculating*.

And don't be afraid to use guilt by association as an analysis tool. If you suspect there are organized-crime–related people or questionable tax-haven banks involved in a scheme, don't wait around until all the evidence is in. Get your money out.

Schemes like J. David will continue to flourish in part because the public remains ignorant. As recently as spring of 1985, San Diego TV stations were routinely referring to Dominelli as a "fallen financier." He was *not* a financier, because he did little investing with the money his customers entrusted to him. He simply took his clients' money and used it for his own purposes.

Similarly, a San Diego columnist in late December told his readers that he felt sorry for Jerry Dominelli; after all, he had given so much to local charities while his operation was succeeding. Obviously, this columnist did not understand that Dominelli was not giving his *own* money to charity. He was being generous with his customers' money. And from a financial standpoint, his operation had never really succeeded. It only stayed in operation until his customers' money, which he had been diverting illegally, ran out.

Amateur psychologists are now having a field day hypothesizing whether Dominelli was mentally unraveling as his firm was financially unraveling. Dominelli stayed absolutely cool when the heat was on. One investor, a doctor, at first interpreted his behavior as an indication of Dominelli's innocence. He later concluded that Dominelli was cool because he was detached from reality. He blamed his downfall on the media and the authorities. That wasn't surprising: The flip side of a con man's delusions of grandeur is paranoia. At the end, investors who had called Dominelli a pathological liar were beginning to think the description might have clinical meaning.

Like many con artists, including Ponzi, Dominelli had come to *believe* in his own scheme. That's one reason he never took off when it was evident J. David was coming asunder. "He went from day to day thinking he could come out of it. He thought he could get ahead of the wave. It had worked so well for so long, the dream would still serve him," says Poovey. In addition to money, the scam gave him another kind of return. Like other con men, he derived great satisfaction from devising a new lie at every crisis point.

The J. David affair was largely a fantasy—a love fantasy. Many say it was a case of *cherchez la femme*—Dominelli turning crooked to win Hoover's heart. A lot of evidence points in that direction. Dominelli apparently concocted his fraudulent track record, for example, to impress Hoover. Hoover was everything Dominelli was not—physically attractive, dynamic, vivacious, sociable, powerful in the community. He lived vicariously through her.

And in selecting handsome, macho salesmen and beautiful secretaries, Dominelli was also living vicariously. For three years he could be their guru—he could fulfill his lifelong dream of giving orders to the Beautiful People, rather than the other way around.

He commanded their respect because they believed he was a financial genius. He may have been diffident and insecure and homely, but he was a genius. Of course, he was a genius in only one respect: "He seems like a nice, simple shit, but he's a devious guy . . . a pro at deceit," says a former J. David consultant.

The fall of J. David wasn't just the crash of a financial house of cards; it was the shattering of one man's fantasies about himself. His so-called genius was his only asset—and it was proved a sham in front of the whole world.

What *was* real was the love affair. Hoover appeared to be as head over heels for Dominelli as he was for her. She wrote him passionate, "grade-schoolish" love letters, according to a former official who found them when rummaging through the remains. "At the end, after the company had collapsed, and they were all engulfed in scandal, they went to dinner. She chewed him out all eve-

235

ning. Do you know why? Because he hadn't committed himself to marrying her," recalls the official. According to one insider, Dominelli got so much heat from Hoover that he arranged to have one of his lawyers tell her that he was working on divorce papers, even though he wasn't.

J. David was a dream that two people shared, and they clung to it even as it went under.

Dominelli's mistake was to run on a track that was too fast for him. He simply did not have the moxie to compete with the pirates who operate out of the Caribbean coves. Evidence suggests that the success of the scheme in fact stunned Dominelli. As the money poured in, even he might have understood that the more that came in, the deeper he would eventually be buried. "When he was sitting there pretending to be trading currencies, I think he was trying to figure out how to get out of the thing," says the former consultant. Of course, he never did figure that out.

The memory will last. J. David is already a legend. Ballpoint pens inscribed with the J. David name are going for $2 to $5 apiece. Robert Mengar turned down a $50 offer for his J. David card-carrying case. At an auction in November 1984, people paid exorbitant prices for items that had belonged to Hoover and Dominelli.

It certainly won't be the last such sale of assets. At the very same time, far north of San Diego, in Moses Lake, Washington, in the heart of the Columbia Basin, another drama was unfolding. One Kenneth D. "Kenny" Oxborrow took his Wheatland Investment Co. into Chapter 11 bankruptcy. The Washington State Department of Licensing and the U.S. CFTC claimed that Oxborrow and Wheatland were not properly registered. Eventually Oxborrow pleaded guilty to defrauding 1,100 investors of $58 million. He is now serving a fifteen-year jail term.

Farmers in the area said that for the previous three years, Oxborrow had been paying his investors 2 to 2.5 percent interest a week—more than 100 percent a year. He told his investors he was putting the money in commodities futures. His neighbors were convinced he had developed a sophisticated, computerized technique for making such astounding returns. What's more, people didn't have to pay any interest if they lost—he just got 20 percent of any profits.

Oxborrow had three airplanes and twelve autos, including a Mercedes-Benz, a Corvette, a Cadillac limousine, and two Rolls-Royces.

People contended he did a lot for the economy of Moses Lake, buying real estate at above-market prices, for example.

Oh, there were cynics. "As a teacher, if I had had to predict what he'd do in life, I would have said he would become a potato-chip driver in Moses Lake," said Arnie Brown, his high-school counselor, explaining that Oxborrow was a C student, although he was "polite, cooperative—I never had a nicer-mannered kid in class."

That's what everybody said. "We heard he was such a Christian man. He had such a good track record," according to a woman in Moses Lake. A farmer observed, "Oxborrow is a nice guy. He did so much for the community. They [the critics] want to kick him when he's down."

Index